AIR RAIDS

WHAT YOU MUST KNOW
WHAT YOU MUST DO!

Edited by John
Christopher

AMBERLEY

Left: The first delivery of Anderson shelters to households in London was made in February 1939, some seven months before the outbreak of war.

First published 2014.

Amberley Publishing
The Hill, Stroud, Gloucestershire, GL5 4EP
www.amberley-books.com

ISBN 978 1 4456 4309 0 (print)
ISBN 978 1 4456 4325 0 (ebook)

British Library Cataloguing in Publication Data.
A catalogue record for this book is available from the British Library.

Typesetting by Amberley Publishing.
Printed in Great Britain.

CONTENTS

INTRODUCTION

There is something almost surreal in many of the illustrations contained in this book. It is the ordinariness of the people, their clothes and homes, the curtains and everyday accoutrements of life, intermingled with the most deadly threat of bombs, poison gas and incendiary devices right in their midst. In a way that had not been seen before on such a scale, the Second World War saw the general public thrown into the thick of it. They were no longer bystanders, although at times they might have felt all but helpless when faced with this onslaught from the skies. Even so, just about everyone did their bit to defy Hitler by carrying on. 'Business as usual' was the familiar notice posted outside newly bombed-out shop premises, and people attempted to carry on their lives, going to the office or the factory, school or hospital, but for millions of them the days were interspersed with civil defence duties. They served as Air Raid Precautions Wardens, spotters spending an eight-hour shift on the rooftops watching for enemy aircraft after a full day's work, fire watchers, and firemen, and let's not forget the Home Guard, of course; the list goes on.

By the time the Luftwaffe's bombers came, the British Government, together with the local authorities, had had some time to make its preparations for Civil Defence. The Air Raids Precautions Committee had been set up as early as 1924, and given the scale of the situation it was understandable that great emphasis was placed on the need for self-reliance on the part of the public. As it says in the

Right: The main content of this book comes from the Ministry of Home Protection publication, *Air Raids – What You Must Know, What You Must Do!* This was a later edition incorporating new guidelines drawn from the experience of the heavy raids in the early stages of the war.

Opposite page: Children in the East End of London sit among the rubble of their homes. (US Library of Congress)

Time and again pictures such as these were published to emphasise the strength of the Anderson shelters and the protection they provided against blast. In the upper photograph, the houses have been severely damaged, while the shleters, protected by their mound of soil, remain intact.

Air Raids booklet issued by the Ministry of Home Security – incidentally it was sold for 3*d* and not given away – 'Civil Defence is everybody's business'. And this policy applied firmly to the question of protecting yourself and your family in the event of an air raid. A key element was knowledge, and that is where this booklet, and other similar publications, played an important role: disseminating the information in an age before television had really taken off. The other aspect of self-protection was the provision of shelter. The best protection was underground, but in crowded areas without public shelters it was a matter of providing a form suitable for individual households.

In February 1938 the Home Secretary appointed a technical committee to look into structural precautions against air attack, and the Anderson shelter was the result. It was designed by William Peterson and Oscar Carl Kerrison, and named after Sir John Anderson, who had had responsibility for preparing air-raid precautions before the outbreak of war. Each one consisted of fourteen panels of galvanised corrugated steel panels. The six main panels bolted together to form the body of the shelter, 6 feet high, 4 feet 6 inches wide and 6 feet 6 inches long. When this was buried up to 4 feet deep in a garden, and covered with a layer of a minimum of 15 inches of soil, it was virtually impregnable to anything but a direct hit. The Anderson shelter was intended to accommodate up to six people, and was issued in flat-pack from February 1939 onwards. The beauty of the design was its simplicity. It was relatively cheap to manufacture in huge quantities, and easy to assemble. They were issued free to all householders who earned less than £5 a week, while those on a higher income had to pay £7. It is estimated that 2.1 million shelters were erected, and at the end of the war the local authorities made arrangements for their removal, or householders could keep them for a nominal fee, which is why so many of the shelters have survived.

The cousin of the corrugated Anderson shelter was the Morrison shelter, this one named after Herbert Morrison, the Minister of Home Security at the time. It was an indoor shelter for houses without a garden space, and took the form of a robust cage strong enough to survive blast damage and the weight of any debris. It came in self-assembly kits to be bolted together, and was 6 feet 6 inches long, 4 feet wide and 2 feet 6 inches high, with a steel framework, solid 'table' top, and wire mesh sides. The relative comfort of being able to stay in your home was negated by the lack of space; there was barely enough room for two people to sleep side by side, and no standing headroom. Without question, both types of shelters saved countless lives.

Aside from the explosive blast of the bombs, the public had to be prepared for the dangers of incendiary devices and the possibility of a gas attack, although thankfully this never materialised. Both of these are covered in this publication, which reproduces the 1941 edition of *Air Raids – What You Must Know, What You Must Do!* It provides a fascinating insight into a time when every man, woman and child was facing the dangers of living on the front line. As stated in the first chapter, 'Information about air raids does not make light or pleasant reading; but it is necessary reading.'

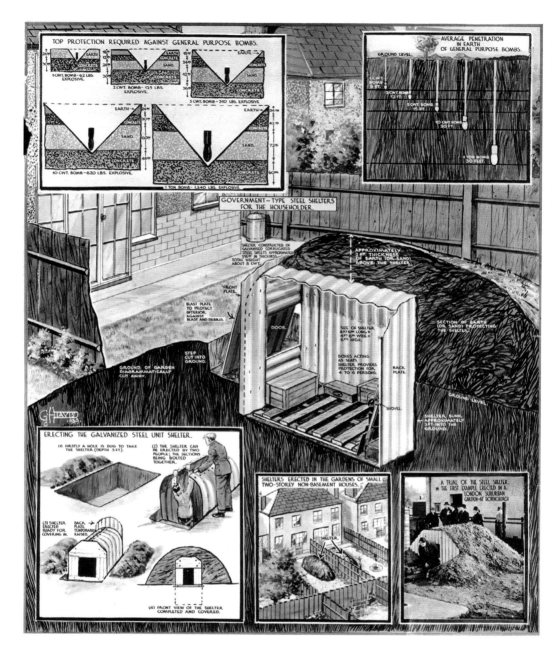

Above: From *The Illustrated London News*, 18 February 1939. 'The ARP department of the Home Office announced its plans for the rapid distribution of steel air raid shelters to small houses throughout London and in twenty-two big cities, on 9 February. Manufacture of the shelters is well in hand and the first supplies are expected to be ready before the end of this month. These shelters are capable of holding from four to six persons. It is hoped eventually to supply them for all houses with not more than two storeys, with sufficient garden space, in all vulnerable areas ... The shelters, are constructed of very strong galvanised corrugated steel sheets, and have been subjected to rigorous tests to ensure their strength when erected to take the weight of any debris that might fall upon them from the type of house for which they are designed. They are made in sections and can be put together by two people without any special skills or experience.'

FOREWORD

TO SECOND EDITION

BY

THE RIGHT HONOURABLE HERBERT MORRISON, M.P.

Minister of Home Security.

This little book needs no words of mine to recommend it to you. It has already had a record sale, exceeding that of any other publication of the Ministry; well over a million copies were sold in less than a year. In its present revised and enlarged form, it embodies new material and new instructions based on the experience gained in the heavy raids of the last few months. This will, I hope, make it even more useful to you all than it was before.

To those of you who live in areas that have already been heavily attacked, I need say only this: Do not weary in well-doing. To those in areas that so far have been more fortunate, I would say: Use the interval to make sure that, if and when the trial comes to you, you will be ready for it—able to protect yourself, and to be of the greatest possible help to your neighbours and to the community.

To all of you I would add this: Keep your knowledge of Air Raid Precautions continually up to date. Thoroughly digest and understand the advice and information that is periodically given to you. New and improved methods of attack call for new forms of defence. We can match the cunning of the enemy only by vigilant development of our precautions and countermeasures. We have recently had to face an intensive form of incendiary attack, and have met it, as you know, by the enrolment of large additional numbers of fire watchers and fire fighters. There will be other developments in the future. We may have to face gas attack; full information is given in these pages about how to act in such an attack and how to help any sufferers from it; and now is the time to make sure you know what to do.

Do *your* part in preparing to meet this and any other form of air attack. Act carefully, calmly, and promptly on the instructions that are given you. Then you may be assured that the new weapons of the enemy, like those he has used so far, will fail to achieve his purpose, while the growth of our own strength will bring ever nearer the day when the last bomb will have fallen and we can begin again to build a world of liberty and peace.

Ministry of Home Security.

September, 1941.

9

LONDON PREPARES : AIR RAID PRECAUTIONS
TAKEN DURING THE CRISIS.

MARKING TREES AND OTHER OBSTRUCTIONS ON THE EMBANKMENT WITH WHITEWASH : PREPARATIONS FOR AN AIR RAID BLACK-OUT IN LONDON. *(Planet.)*

TO WARN PASSENGERS OF ANY IMPENDING AIR RAID : EMERGENCY LOUD-SPEAKERS BEING INSTALLED ON MOBILE TROLLEYS AT LIVERPOOL STREET STATION. *(Keystone.)*

" CLOSED FOR URGENT STRUCTURAL WORKS " : THE UNDERGROUND STATION AT WATERLOO WITH THE ENTRANCE SHUT — ONE OF SEVERAL LONDON STATIONS THUS CLOSED. *(C.P.)*

AIR RAID PRECAUTIONS IN THE CITY OF LONDON : THE HEAVILY SANDBAGGED ENTRANCE TO SNOW HILL POLICE-STATION DURING THE CRISIS. *(Wide World.)*

WITH AIR-BELLOWS WHICH ARE OPERATED BY THE MOVEMENT OF THE PET WITHIN : A GAS-PROOF CHAMBER FOR ANIMALS. *(Fox.)*

ADVISING PEOPLE WHERE TO GO TO GET THEIR GAS MASKS FITTED : A PUBLICITY DRIVE BY POSTER AND LOUD-SPEAKER VAN IN WESTMINSTER. *(A.P.)*

Above: Photo feature on the ARP measures introduced in October 1938, at the time of the Munich Crisis. They include painting stripes on trees and street furniture to aid in the blackout, as well as additional warning speakers at stations, sandbag protection of public buildings, a gas-proof shelter for animals produced by the PDSA, and a mobile information campaign about gas mask use.

CHAPTER 1

CIVILIANS AND CIVIL DEFENCE.

Civil Defence is still a comparatively new subject. It has come into being because of a new kind of war—a war in which the enemy tries to disrupt the whole of civilian life by air attack, as well as to destroy military targets.

That is why Civil Defence is everybody's business. It not only requires the valour and skill of the Civil Defence Services; it not only needs the inventiveness of the scientists who are constantly at work on security problems; but it depends in the last instance on the commonsense of the ordinary, sensible folk who take the trouble to find out beforehand what is likely to happen in air raids, what they themselves ought to do about it, and how the nation's Civil Defence system has been planned to help them do it.

For war purposes the country has been divided into twelve regions, each with a Regional Commissioner appointed by the King. One object of this regionalisation is to ensure that in an emergency—for instance, after a heavy raid—urgent steps that are necessary in the public interest can be taken at once and urgent questions settled on the spot, without the delay that would be bound to happen if every matter had to be referred to London.

Each Regional Commissioner is responsible among other matters for the efficiency of Civil Defence organisation throughout his region, and for the co-ordination of after-raid measures. He is answerable in these matters to the Ministry of Home Security. He has the help of a team of Regional Officers representing other Government departments.

Under the general direction and supervision of the Regional Commissioner, Civil Defence is in the hands of the local authorities. The local Civil Defence services are the responsibility of a Civil Defence Controller, assisted by a Civil Defence Officer.

At this stage of the war most people are familiar with the network of the Civil Defence Services themselves. There are first of all the Wardens, who are the essential link between the public and the Civil Defence Services, and who are responsible for advising and helping their neighbours on all Civil Defence matters, and for reporting damage and "incidents" and summoning the appropriate help. Then there are the messengers, clerks and telephonists who staff the Report Centres from which the dispatch of the various services is organised; there are the Rescue and Demolition Parties and Decontamination Squads; the First Aid Parties and Ambulance Drivers and Attendants; and the doctors, nurses and first-aiders who man the First Aid Posts. Finally, there is the vast organisation for wartime defence against fire: the Auxiliary Fire Service, formed to reinforce the regular fire brigades and now incorporated with them in the National Fire Service; and the hundreds of thousands of Fire Guards enrolled in recent months and now organised for fire prevention all over the country as part of the Wardens' Service.

This great army of Civil Defence workers, whose numbers amount to millions, has been chiefly built up and is still chiefly dependent on voluntary civilian effort. It is at the same time a remarkably efficient and indomitable army; a "Fourth Arm" of defence, of which the nation is justly proud.

It is, however, not enough to be proud of the Civil Defence Services. There is one way in which every civilian ought to be ready actively to help in organised Civil Defence: and that is by being as ready as possible to help himself.

In the crisis of a heavy raid there is always a percentage of people in acute distress, and a large number of people with real but very much lesser worries. At such a time the hard-pressed Civil Defence organisation needs to be free to give help where it is needed most. The people who can look after their own smaller troubles and perhaps do something to help and advise others are the Civil Defence workers' best friends; whereas the people who clutter up the police and the telephone wires with their not very urgent personal difficulties are definitely delaying the help that is needed by people in much greater danger and distress.

A great deal of muddle can be avoided by collecting a few addresses in good time: the address of the nearest Wardens' Post, the nearest First Aid Post and the local "Information" or "Administrative" Centre where advice on all post-raid problems is obtainable immediately after a raid. The best plan in the case of being bombed out is to have a "mutual hospitality" arrangement made beforehand with a relative or friend—based on the understanding that whichever one is bombed out will go to the one who is not; and based too on the hope that both will not be bombed out together. If a "mutual hospitality" arrangement is not possible, it is important to find out before the raid the address of the nearest Rest Centre where temporary accommodation and food will be available for homeless people.

The next step towards self-reliance is to get a background of elementary knowledge about air raids: what the enemy is trying to do, what methods and weapons he is using, how to counter his attack by finding out in advance as much as possible about his wicked game. It is no use beginning to get interested in the technique of air raids and Civil Defence once the raid is on. The time to acquire useful information is beforehand.

That means absorbing some rather dull details and pondering quite a number of very unsavoury facts. Information about air raids does not make light or pleasant reading; but it is necessary information. The Nazis have been using their evil ingenuity for years to plan this aerial attack on civilians. Therefore civilians must rely on their brains as well as their good intentions, and summon their commonsense as well as their courage if the defence of civilian life is to be adequate.

CHAPTER 2

INCENDIARY BOMBS AND FIRE PRECAUTIONS.

I. Description of a Fire Bomb.

By far the most effective incendiary agent used in air raids is the small "kilo" or 2¼ lb. magnesium bomb, which has a shell or casing of magnesium alloy and a core of thermite priming composition.

When the fire bomb strikes a hard surface such as a tiled roof the impact operates a fuse which ignites the thermite core of the bomb. This burns at a very high temperature and quickly ignites the magnesium shell or casing, which then burns fiercely with intense heat. There is some spluttering for about a minute, during which burning metal may be thrown as far as 30 feet and will set fire to anything within reach. After this the bomb collapses into a small pool of molten metal which continues to burn with intense heat, but without spluttering, for about 10 minutes.

Some fire bombs have a small explosive charge which may burst shortly after impact—usually within the first two minutes. Pieces of burning magnesium and steel fragments are then thrown in all directions. The steel splinters are capable of causing deadly wounds at close quarters, and serious wounds at 30 feet.

II. How to Fight Fire Bombs.

Small fire bombs are so compact and light that one aeroplane can carry many hundreds of them so that even if many are wasted, there may still be enough to cause numbers of fires in any one area. During a concentrated incendiary attack, therefore, it is essential for the bombs to be dealt with promptly and as far as possible smothered as soon as they fall. Fighting fires that have taken a hold is a job for the fire brigade, but fighting fire bombs —and so preventing fires—is essentially a job for the ordinary citizen; otherwise the fires that can be started in an incendiary attack will prove far too numerous and extensive for any fire brigade organisation or any water supply to deal with.

Tackling a fire bomb is a fairly simple matter for those who know how. It is a job that requires speed and some training. A burning fire bomb cannot be dealt with in the same way as an ordinary source of fire. To throw a bucket of water over a fire bomb or play a small jet of water on it is dangerous because this will make the bomb splutter more and molten metal will be thrown in all directions. Neither are fire extinguishers so generally useful as stirrup pumps for dealing with fire bombs and the contents of some fire extinguishers when thrown on fire bombs will generate poisonous fumes.

When a fire bomb falls in the open the best method of dealing with it is to smother it with dry sand, earth or ashes. These will not normally put the bomb out—it may continue to burn underneath for some time—but they will reduce the heat and glare and spluttering, and so prevent the bomb from setting fire to things around it. The easiest way to use sand, earth or ash for this purpose is in *sandbags* or *sandmats*; and the authorities have distributed large numbers of these in the streets and to householders.

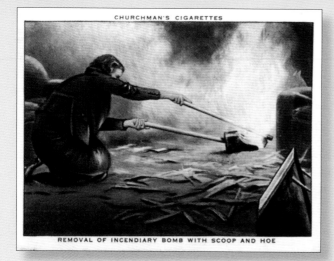

REMOVAL OF INCENDIARY BOMB WITH SCOOP AND HOE

Air-Raid Precautions, a series of cigarette cards issued by Imperial Tobacco and given away with packs of Churchman cigarettes. The colourful cards were a clever way of promulgating the information in a popular way and in easily digested bite-size chunks.

Above and right: Two cards on dealing with an incendiary bomb that has landed in your sitting room. The scoop and hoe are used draw the bomb into the scoop. The two parts are then joined together to create a long handle and the bomb is deposited in a Redhill Container, which is designed to be carried in safety without risk of burning the carrier's hand. 'Householders who have acquired the little training necessary to deal with these bombs will help in a great measure to defeat the enemy's object.'

EXTINCTION OF INCENDIARY BOMB

TWO-MEN PORTABLE MANUAL FIRE-PUMP IN ACTION

Left: The two-man, or in this case two-woman, manual pump in action was intended for tackling small fires. The portable canvas tank from which the pump draws water could be replenished from dometic water supplies, such as a bath or tap.

Right: 'Medium trailer fire-pumps will be an important feature in emergency fire-brigade measures. These are towed behind private cars or commercial vans (in which the firemen and gear may be carried), and can be man-handled over rough ground or debris impassible to ordinary fire engines or motor cars. A pump of this type will give four good streams of water at high pressure.'

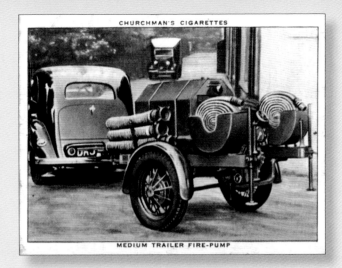

MEDIUM TRAILER FIRE-PUMP

Middle right: Light trailer fire-pumps were issued to many local authorities. Lighter than the medium pump, it too could be towed by a vehicle or manhandled, and was capable of delivering two streams of water, up to 120 gallons per minute, at a pressure of 80 lbs to the square inch.

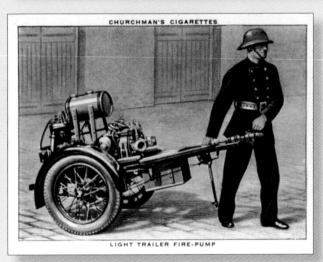

LIGHT TRAILER FIRE-PUMP

Bottom right: 'During an air raid, alternative supplies of water may be required should water mains be damaged by exploding bombs. For laying long lines of delivery hose, such as may be necessary at large fire for the purpose of utilising distant water supplies, the lengths of hose are joined together and specially packed in the hose-laying lorry shown here.'

HOSE-LAYING LORRY

When a bomb falls in the open . . .

Hold a sandmat in front of your face . . .

Place it on the bomb . . .

and get away *quickly.*

A sandbag should be about half full of dry sand, earth or ashes, which should be shaken evenly through the bag. It is a good idea to tie the corners with string to form "ears" so that the bag can be grasped easily.

A sandmat has the advantage of being lighter to handle. It is made by cutting an ordinary standard sandbag in half, filling the half with 20 lbs. of dry sand, earth or ash and then sewing it up. This makes a loose cushion which can be grasped in the middle by one hand, so that the fingers are not exposed.

Sandbags and sandmats should be kept as dry as possible. The sand should not be emptied out on to the bomb nor should the sandbag or sandmat be thrown at the bomb, but placed on it squarely; and once the bomb is smothered it is as well to get right away quickly for fear of explosion.

When a fire bomb falls indoors it is usually best tackled with a *stirrup pump*

How to enter a burning room.

The pump operator stays outside room.

Keep under cover as you attack bomb.

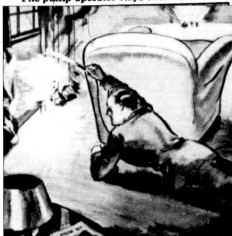
First check fire *caused* by fire bomb.

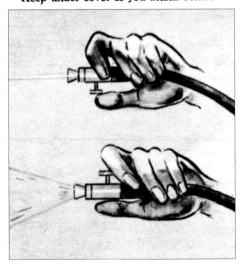

A fire bomb may, of course, fall indoors on a non-inflammable surface where sand can cover it at once; but ordinarily a fire bomb falling indoors will land on an inflammable surface such as a wood floor or lath and plaster ceiling and very likely set furniture and hangings alight immediately; and sand, is in these circumstances of very little use for checking the fire either under the bomb or round it. The advantage of the stirrup pump is that it can deal with both the fire and the bomb.

The stirrup pump is a simple hand pump. The shaft is placed in a bucket of water and held steady by a foot grip outside. The pump has about 30 feet of hose, with a dual purpose nozzle at the end to give either a jet of water carrying about 30 feet or a fine spray reaching about 15 feet. When the stirrup pump is used to tackle a burning bomb and surrounding fire the jet and the spray are used alternatively—the jet on the fire and the spray on the bomb (the change-over is made in a second by the simple operation of a slide). The jet, though small, is stronger than it looks, and with energetic pumping it will put out a considerable fire.. The spray when played on the bomb does not increase the spluttering as a jet of water would do, but has the effect of speeding up combustion by supplying oxygen, so that the bomb burns out in about 1 minute instead of 10.

The stirrup pump requires about 6 gallons of water to control a small bomb and extinguish a fire in a room of medium size and average furnishings.

This pump can be used effectively by two people or even in an emergency, by one; but it is best operated by three people working in a team as follows :—

No. 1 leads the party, takes the nozzle, and tackles the bomb and fire.

No. 2 does the pumping, going slowly when pressure on the pump indicates that the spray is being used and faster when the jet is being used.

No. 3 brings up fresh supplies of water, watches for any spread of the fire and relieves Nos. 1 and 2 as necessary.

When there are only two people, one takes the nozzle and the other sees to the pumping and the water supply.

Nos. 2 and 3 of a stirrup pump team go no nearer the fire than necessary. No. 1 with the nozzle should go forward carefully, taking advantage of any available cover such as a door or upturned table. If the room is full of smoke he should crawl along the floor, as the air will be clearer near the ground. Usually he will find it best to deal first with the fire caused by the bomb so as to clear the air and make it easier to get at the bomb. Then he should change from the jet, and use the spray on the bomb, going gradually nearer until he is attacking it from a distance of about six feet. He should alternate between the bomb and the surrounding fire until both are put out.

Afterwards burnt articles such as furniture and cushions should be raked over to make sure they are not still smouldering, and a careful search made, if necessary under floor boards and panelling in case the fire may have crept unnoticed into out-of-the-way corners.

A stirrup pump is often very useful for dealing with bombs in awkward places, whether indoors or out. When a bomb is quite inaccessible a long-handled rake may be a help.

The most important fire bombs are usually those which fall on or inside or behind buildings, and not those which fall in the street or in an open space. People who rush out of doors to deal with comparatively harmless fire bombs may return to find their houses well alight. Special watch should be kept for fire bombs in and on buildings, and normally these bombs should be dealt with first. Bombs that fall in the open will often burn themselves out harmlessly, though if they have fallen where they can obviously start a fire—for instance, next a petrol tank—they must of course be tackled at once. In deciding which fire bomb to tackle first it should be remembered that though isolated incendiaries in the open may make a dangerous glare for a few minutes, a burning building makes a much more dangerous glare and for a much longer time.

Unignited incendiary bombs are not dangerous if handled carefully. They should either be dropped into water or handed at once to the Police, Fire Services or Military or A.R.P. authorities, or else reported to them and left on the open ground to be collected.

Precautions against Explosive Fire Bombs and Fragments of Ordinary Fire Bombs.

When a fire bomb is burning there is no way of telling whether it will explode or not, but there is little risk of explosion when the bomb has been burning more than two minutes. Fire bombs that fall in the open or in other places where they are not likely to set fire to anything else can usually be left to burn for two minutes before being dealt with. Fire bombs that fall indoors will usually have been burning for at least two minutes by the time the stirrup pump and other equipment are brought along to put them out.

All the same there are some fire bombs that have to be tackled immediately, and whether a fire bomb has an explosive charge in it or not, it is liable to splutter at first. Anyone approaching it therefore should use what cover he can. If he has a sandmat he should hold it in front of his face till he gets up to the bomb, then smother the bomb and get away quickly. If he is No. 1 of a stirrup pump party he should go forward sideways and shelter if possible behind a door or piece of furniture while playing the hose on the fire. If he is No. 2 or No. 3 of the party he should keep as far from the fire as the length of the hose allows—preferably outside the burning room.

Tests have shown that almost complete protection against explosive fire bombs and against flying molten metal can be obtained at all distances with a shield of $\frac{7}{8}$ in. board not less than 28 ins. long and 20 ins. wide and backed with 22 gauge mild steel. The shield should have two peepholes 1 in. wide and $\frac{3}{16}$ in. deep, one midway between the two sides and not less than 5 in. from the top, the other not more than 18 ins. from the bottom, with the centre point not less than 8 ins. from one side. At one side of the shield there should be a slot $3\frac{1}{2}$ ins. long and $1\frac{1}{2}$ ins. wide for the nozzle of the stirrup hand pump. The shield should have a handle fixed to the back and long enough for the shield to be held upright by anyone crouching while approaching a bomb or lying prone with one elbow resting on the ground.

This shield weighs about 15 lbs. and is therefore too heavy for the average householder. It is useful chiefly to industrial fire parties operating in buildings of high fire risk. There are, however, various lighter shields which give useful protection, for example:

(1) A solid or built-up $\frac{7}{8}$ in. board backed by a dustbin lid or beaten-out corrugated iron or other thin plate gives a large measure of protection.

(2) A $\frac{1}{2}$ in. board similarly backed, or a $\frac{1}{16}$ in. steel plate, gives full protection against flying pieces of burning magnesium and flying sand or soil, but is not completely proof against penetration by flying steel splinters at 15 feet (the maximum distance at which spray from a stirrup pump can be effectively used on a burning bomb).

(3) A $\frac{1}{4}$ in. ply board, or a dustbin lid, or four thicknesses of folded wet blanket hung in front of the face over one arm gives full protection against molten magnesium and flying sand or soil but not against steel splinters even at a greater distance than 15 feet.

Failing anything better a dustbin lid will protect the face and head against molten magnesium and flying sand or soil, but it is quite ineffective against steel fragments.

Right: Front Line 1940–41 told the official story of the work of the Civil Defence and was published by HMSO during the war itself, in 1942. It covered all aspects of Civil Defence including the stirling endeavours of the fire fighters. The Auxiliary Fire Service (AFS) was formed in 1938 to supplement the local fire brigades. The main image shows fires raging in Ave Maria Lane in the East End of London, December 1940.

III. The Work of the Fire Guard.

Incendiary raids are essentially indiscriminate. They are a general threat to the very life of the nation. They must be answered not by spasmodic individual efforts but by a network of trained fire parties covering all vulnerable areas. This national fire prevention service has now been organised as Britain's Fire Guard.

The men and women who make up the Fire Guard form an integral part of the Wardens' Service, and are organised in fire parties under their own officers and N.C.O.s. The work of the Fire Guard is to watch for fire bombs and deal with as many as possible as soon as they come down, so that fires do not get a hold. In areas prescribed by the Regional Commissioners occupiers of all business premises are required to make appropriate fire prevention arrangements. In residential areas the usual plan is to have one Fire Guard party in charge of a sector of about 150 yards. Fire prevention began as voluntary service, and the fact that in vulnerable areas there is now a compulsory Fire Guard scheme for residential as well as business premises, in no way diminishes the vital necessity for all volunteer Fire Guards, including women, to continue their fine work.

Throughout the blackout, whether there is an alert or not, Fire Guards, dressed and ready for action, are on duty in every street in the residential portions of all urban areas. Streets are divided into sectors and in each sector the Fire Guards are so organised as to provide at all times during the blackout a duty party consisting of three persons. Throughout the blackout one of these three Fire Guards is standing by; the two other members of the duty party are permitted to undress and get to bed until it is time for them to relieve the Fire Guard on duty. The Fire Guard on duty is required at all times to be ready to start watching as soon as the alert is sounded or at the approach of hostile aircraft if, for any reason, this should precede the sounding of the alert. Immediately on the sounding of the alert, the Fire Guard on duty has to keep careful watch for the fall of fire bombs. At this stage, however, he is *not* required to wake the two other members of his duty party. If he considers that there is imminent danger (i.e. if he hears gunfire in the neighbourhood or the fall of bombs), the Fire Guard on duty has then to rouse the two other members of his duty party, who at once dress and await the next stage. This next stage is reached when fire bombs actually begin to fall in the neighbourhood. At this stage, the Fire Guard on duty blows his whistle, and at this signal the two other members of his duty party, who, by now are ready for action, come out to help to deal with the fire bombs.

It will be realised that in order to maintain each night a duty party for each street (or part of a street) of three Fire Guards, it is necessary to form a considerably larger group, the members of which, in parties of three, take it in turns to form the duty party on particular nights. Once fire bombs actually begin to fall, all the Fire Guards who form part of this larger group for the street in question who happen to be at home at the time, are expected to dress as quickly as possible and to turn out to assist the duty party, the members of which, up till now, had alone been on duty that night. These other Fire Guards operate in the same parties of three as those to which they belong on those nights when they themselves constitute the duty party. In effect these Fire Guards constitute reserve duty parties, which begin to function as soon as fire bombs start to fall.

A smaller number of persons is required to be on duty at any particular time if "key watchers" are organised, that is to say, if there is a system by which one watcher occupies a vantage point, which either commands a good view of the roof area or is situated at a cross road which commands a view down four streets. One watcher in such a position can act for several duty parties, but should have means of communication (e.g. by telephone) with the Fire Guard on duty for that night belonging to each of the duty parties for whom he acts as key-watcher. If no telephone is available, the key-watcher on bombs beginning to fall, leaves his post to call the Fire Guard on duty belonging to the nearest of the duty parties. Directly he has done so, it is his duty to return to his post and resume watching. It is the duty of the Fire Guard whom he has aroused to arouse the Fire Guards on duty belonging to the other duty parties concerned.

Two stirrup pumps are supplied by the local authority to each of the street sectors referred to above, to supplement those privately owned by the Fire Guards comprised in the group who take nightly turns in manning that sector.

IV. Household Precautions against Fire.

Successful fire prevention depends very largely on what help the Fire Guards get from people living in their sector. Householders who cannot themselves join the Fire Guard should co-operate in every possible way. The most important household precautions are these:

(1) Have ready a supply of water in the bath and in buckets and let the Fire Guards know where to find it. Used bath water economises on the water supply. During cold weather keep the water where it will not freeze. Householders should also provide containers holding 4 gallons of water, immediately outside or inside the main entrance of their houses. One of these containers should be capable of being used with a stirrup hand pump.

(2) Have ready supplies of earth or sand, a shovel, a hatchet, and if possible a ladder or "steps" and a rake. Keep sand mats on each landing and the other things together on the ground floor. Again, tell the Fire Guards where they are.

(3) If you have a stirrup pump put a sign "S.P." in your window (this sign is obtainable from the local authority), and tell the Fire Guards how to get the pump whether you are at home or not.

(4) See that as many members of your family as possible get practical training in dealing with fire bombs, both with the stirrup pump and with sandbags. Local demonstrations are arranged for this purpose.

(5) When you go away turn off gas and electricity at the main. Leave the curtains of upstairs rooms pulled back, so that a fire inside could be seen from the street.

(6) See that you and members of your family know where to get the Warden and Fire Brigade. Fire bombs are the chief, but not the only fire danger during raids. If an oil-bomb hits your house it will probably catch fire. There is also a risk of fire from the effects of high explosives (see page 20).

(7) Clear your attics, lofts and roof spaces of everything inflammable. This is a legal requirement under the Defence Regulations in all urban areas, and it applies to all lofts and attics except those used for human habitation and those which are accessible by a fixed staircase.

V. Strengthening of Roofs and Protection of Roof Spaces.

One obvious way to protect a building against fire bombs is to strengthen the roof.

The small magnesium incendiary bomb will penetrate any ordinary roof

Rescuing an insensible person from a burning room.

Bringing an insensible person downstairs.

material, such as slate or tiles or corrugated iron. If there is a lath-and-plaster ceiling immediately below the roof the bomb will usually penetrate or burn through it, and fall on the floor. If the floor is boarded, the bomb will soon burn through the boards or molten metal from the bomb will trickle through them and set fire to the room beneath.

Protection against large incendiary bombs is not easy, but protection against small kilo bombs can be arranged. A flat roof, provided the rafters are strong enough, may be covered with protective material. Particulars relating to such materials have been published in the technical press and householders should consult their builders or their local authority, who will be in possession of the necessary information.

Where there is a hipped roof of tiles or slates or corrugated iron, the best plan is to protect or reinforce the floor immediately under the roof, and increase the fire resistance of the rafters by painting them with fire-resisting paint or material as described below. Where the attic floor is not already boarded, the householder should consult his builder or his local authority.

There are various ways of increasing the fire-resistance of rafters. They may be covered with a mixture made of 24 ozs. of kaolin (china clay) and 18 ozs. of sodium silicate in syrup form, mixed with one pint of water. Alternatively the rafters may be well covered with one of the many fire-resisting paints or plasters now obtainable, but a commercial preparation of this kind should not be used unless it conforms to the official specification. (British Standard Specification, A.R.P. 39.)

Painting does not make the rafters entirely fire-proof, but it will prolong the resistance of the woodwork and so give time for the bomb to be tackled before it sets fire to its surroundings. Any method of fire-proofing rafters would, however, be largely ineffective if the roof space had not been cleared of all inflammable materials.

VI. Escape and Rescue.

Every one should be familiar with the following general rules :

(1) When searching a house for its occupants, start at the top and work downwards.

(2) When fighting a fire, escaping from fire or saving others, lie down and crawl to avoid smoke and heat.

(3) Do not use burning passages or stairways when rescue can be effected through the window.

(4) If you have to use a burning stairway or passage or cross a burning room, keep near the walls where there is greater support for the floor.

(5) To move an unconscious person along the floor, lay him on his back, tie his wrists together, then kneel astride him, put your head through the loop of his arms and, taking his weight round your neck, crawl forward slowly on your hands and knees.

(6) To move an unconscious person downstairs, put him face uppermost at the top of the stairs with his head towards the bottom, then support him under his armpits and move slowly backwards downstairs.

(7) If your clothing is on fire, clap your hands over your mouth, lie down and roll over and over on the floor.

(8) If someone else's clothing is on fire, hold a blanket or overcoat in front of yourself, throw the other person on the ground, throw the

Preparing to escape from an upstairs window.

Dropping from an upstairs window.

blanket or coat over him and then roll him over and over until the flames are put out.

(9) Keep doors and windows closed as much as possible in a burning building, to restrict the supply of fresh air to the fire. If you have to go into a burning room of which the door opens outwards, put your foot a few inches back from the closed door to control the swing, so that you can open the door steadily and use it as a shield against the outrush of flame, hot gas and smoke. Then drop to your knees and if necessary crawl in, keeping close to the walls.

(10) To escape from a window when there is no rope, put your legs outside and sit on the sill, then turn over with your stomach on the sill so as to face the wall, lower your body to the full extent of your arms and drop with knees bent.

25

CHAPTER 3

HIGH EXPLOSIVES.

I. Types of High Explosive Bombs.

High explosive bombs vary in length from a few inches to as much as 14 ft. and may weigh anything from about 4 lbs. to about 4,000. Apart from bombs designed for use against special targets, a high explosive bomb consists usually of a relatively thin steel case containing a charge of high explosive mixture and fitted with a fuse and exploder. When the fuse operates the explosive mixture inside the bomb is converted into hot and greatly compressed gases which burst the bomb case.

The smaller high explosives, about the size of coffee tins, are *anti-personnel bombs*. After explosion the fragments of these bombs are projected at a tremendous velocity. Anti-personnel bombs are highly dangerous to human beings though not to buildings, and if found unexploded they are liable to burst as soon as handled (see page 22).

The *general purpose bombs* most commonly used in air bombardment weigh from about 100 to about 4,000 lbs. They have a very high explosive content and are extremely destructive in built-up areas.

Instantaneous and Delay-action Fuses.

The flight of the bomb after its release from the aircraft is steadied by means of a tail unit, fitted with vanes or fins, and the explosive charge is detonated by a fuse which operates when the bomb hits a hard surface, or at a set interval afterwards.

An *instantaneous fuse* causes a bomb to explode immediately on impact with the ground or other hard surface. A *normal delay-action fuse* introduces a brief time interval between impact and explosion. This interval, which varies according to the fuse setting, is usually from a fraction of a second to a few seconds, and so gives the bomb time to penetrate deeply into a building or other objective before exploding. A *long delay fuse* is based on the same principle but introduces a much longer time interval between impact and explosion—sometimes a period of hours or even days. The presence of long-delay-action bombs or "time" bombs therefore calls for special precautions (see page 22).

II. Effects of High Explosive Bombs.

Earth Shock. A high explosive bomb penetrating the ground sets up a shock wave in the earth itself, and this concussive force—a kind of localised earthquake—can be felt in buildings near the point of impact. Earth shock may be severe enough not only to damage water pipes and other utility services in the earth, but to cause the collapse of walls and chimney stacks, and other structural damage to buildings.

The way a building stands up to earth shock depends largely on the resilience or elasticity in the building itself: a principle which has been applied with outstanding success in the designing of "Anderson" shelters and the new surface shelters.

Blast. Blast is the shock wave that travels through the air after an explosion The effect of the explosion is sudden pressure on the surrounding air, followed

26

by suction. The shock wave thus created travels at tremendous speed until the energy of the wave is spent. In the immediate vicinity of the bomb both pressure and suction are very violent and are sufficient to damage and demolish buildings. The direct effects of blast on the human body are, on the whole, much less severe. The impact of the blast wave on the body wall may cause bruising of the lungs and sometimes other organs, but serious or fatal injury directly attributable to blast is likely only very near indeed to the bomb. The view that blast causes internal injury by forcing its way into the body through the mouth and nose, or sucking air out through the mouth and nose, has been discredited. Distant effects of blast are often seen in damage to the lighter parts of buildings: balconies, roof tiles and slates, ceiling plaster and window panes.

The behaviour of blast varies according to the size of the bomb and other factors, and often seems to have freakish results. This is due to the combined and contradictory effects of pressure and suction, and to the way the blast wave may be deflected from walls and other unyielding surfaces.

The object of the blast walls and "baffles" erected for the protection of many buildings is to reduce the force of the shock wave by putting obstacles in its path, and to interrupt and deflect it.

Splinters. The bursting of a high explosive bomb breaks the bomb case into thousands of jagged metal splinters which fly upwards and outwards at terrific speed. Most of these splinters are small—not more than 1 in. across —but they are very dangerous: having great penetrative power even at a distance, because of the force with which they are thrown. They have in fact been known to cause fatal injury half a mile away from a bomb explosion. Sometimes they come from unexpected directions because they have been deflected by a wall or other hard surface.

It has been proved that though bomb splinters can penetrate 2 ins. of mild steel plate, they are unlikely to go more than 30 ins. into a bank of sand or rampart of sand-bags.

Fire. Even when high explosive bombs are not accompanied by incendiaries, the high explosives themselves may cause serious outbreaks of fire. When this happens it is usually because gas-pipes have been fractured or because debris has fallen where an ordinary domestic fire has set light to it.

To minimise these risks it is important to turn off gas at the main during raids and when leaving home, to keep coal fires damped down during raids, and above all to be familiar with the fire prevention measures outlined in Chapter 2 (see particularly pages 14 and 15). The danger of fire even in the absence of incendiaries, reinforces the urgency of all fire prevention measures in air raids.

III. General Protective Measures against High Explosives

The subject of shelter is dealt with in Chapter 4, and a chart on page 29 shows to what extent the risk of injury is reduced by different forms of cover. Even when shelter is not available there are various simple precautions that may prevent injury or save life during an air bombardment.

Falling Flat. The most important fact to remember is that when a bomb bursts, the blast, splinters and debris all tend to fly outwards and upwards. Therefore if high explosive bombs are whistling down and shelter is not available, it is better to be in a hollow (even in the gutter) than on the level, and it is better to crouch down or lie flat than to stand up. The safest position is lying face downwards, resting on the elbows, hands clasped behind the

Rescue Squads

They are the unsung heroes of the Home Front of the Second World War. The RSDs, the Rescue, Shoring & Demolition Squads, set to work after an air raid to rescue victims of the bombing. Through the night they were hard at work propping dangerous structures as they tunnelled underneath to reach people who were trapped beneath the rubble. It was arduous and difficult work, fraught with danger, but without them many victims would have suffocated or maybe drowned in the waters of a burst main. In London these civilians were enlisted by the County Council, and most were building labourers, carpenters or demolition workers.

These photographs, showing a real rescue, were published in November 1940.

head, and chest slightly raised from the ground to prevent internal injury from earth shock.

Protection near buildings and under other cover. A wall or archway may give protection from bomb splinters and debris as well as from the fragments of shrapnel and spent fragments that accompany an anti-aircraft barrage; but whether indoors or out, it must be remembered that shock transmitted through walls or earthwork can cause serious internal injury, and that it may be extremely dangerous to lean *direct* against any part of a building or trench. A cushion or rolled up coat gives protection.

Failing any substantial cover, the head and other vital parts of the body should be protected in any way possible, for instance with a thick rug or coat or even an open book.

The Safest Part of a Room. Indoors it is better to be near an inside wall than an outside one, and to avoid being in a direct line with the door or window. One of the chief dangers is from flying glass splinters. Windows offer less resistance to blast, and are therefore less likely to be shattered if they are left open; and it is only during a gas attack that they must be kept closed. Protective treatments for windows are dealt with on page 26).

Protecting the Ear-drums. The ear-drums are liable to be injured by blast. They can be protected by small pads of cotton wool, which should be smeared with vaseline if possible, and packed loosely into the ears. This reduces noise as well as shock. An alternative is to use the rubber ear-plugs which are now issued free to the public. These should be moistened and then inserted in a slightly upward direction into the ear canal with a gentle screwing movement. They can be shortened if necessary by having slices cut off the narrow end. Earplugs should be wiped over after use and kept clean.

Precautions at Home after the Raid. People living in a neighbourhood where high explosives have fallen should make a careful examination of their houses—roofs, walls, windows and doors—even if there are no obvious signs of damage. Any structural defects caused by the raid should be reported to the local A.R.P. authority and the house should be left at once if it seems unsafe. Temporary repairs needed to make the house wind and waterproof will be arranged by the local authority.

Damage to electric, gas and water supplies is probable. It should be remembered that the local public utility services are responsible only for the services in the roads outside and that the conduits, meters and pipes inside the house are the concern of the owner or tenant. Householders whose electric, water or gas supplies are damaged inside the house should therefore not look for immediate help to the local public utility repair squads but should themselves make arrangements for temporary repairs.

If there is damage to the electric conduits, the supply should be kept switched off at the main switch. If a gas pipe is damaged, the supply should be kept cut off at the meter or at an intermediate tap until repairs are done, unless it is possible to plug up the pipe with wood or soap. If a water pipe is broken, the supply should be kept off at the main stopcock until the pipe can be plugged, otherwise there may be serious flooding. A leak from a water pipe or gas pipe made of lead can be stopped by flattening the end of the pipe, and bending over the flattened part.

If the water supply is cut off from outside the water in the storage tank must be used very economically and chiefly for drinking purposes after having been boiled. The hot water boiler fire must be kept out until the supply is restored. Any official instructions to boil water before using it should be observed most carefully. Under air raid conditions it is important to use as little water as possible because of the shortage likely from damage to mains and the urgent needs of the fire brigade and other services.

IV. Precautions against Unexploded Bombs and Shells.

Unexploded anti-personnel bombs may be found on or very near the surface of the earth.

They are usually small (length 3¼ ins., diameter 3¼ ins.) and of a black-lead grey colour. They may be alone or attached to a short wire cable and a kind of metal parachute.

They are liable to explode and cause serious injury if they are handled or subjected to vibration. They should therefore be left alone and at a distance, and reported to an A.R.P. warden or to the police.

Delay-action general purpose bombs. When a bomb comes down without exploding it just makes a thud, no smoke is given off, no flash is seen, and the smell of gases that ordinarily follows a bomb explosion is absent.

Whereas when a bomb hits the ground and explodes, it makes a funnel-shaped crater with splashes of earth around, an unexploded bomb makes no crater but buries itself in the earth, sometimes to a great depth, leaving only a comparatively small circular hole to show where it has gone in. What at first may look like a small crater formed by a very small bomb may be the entrance hole of a large unexploded bomb, and should therefore be avoided.

Bombs that come down without exploding are of two kinds. Either they are "dud" bombs which because of some defect will probably never explode; or they are delay-action bombs ("time" bombs) which will explode at a set interval, whether of minutes, hours or days, after they come down. There being nothing by which the ordinary person can distinguish the safe "dud" bomb from the dangerous "time" bomb, it is wise to assume that any unexploded bomb may be dangerous.

People who have been temporarily evacuated on account of unexploded bombs should not try to go back to their homes on foolish errands. Anyone who thinks he has heard an unexploded bomb come down should tell an A.R.P. warden or policeman. Anyone looking for an unexploded bomb should move very carefully, as vibration may make it go off. Anyone finding an unexploded bomb should on no account handle it, but should report it at once to a warden or to the police.

Unexploded shells, fired by anti-aircraft guns or by aircraft, are liable to be found lying about after an air-raid. They can be recognised by the copper driving band in front of the base, and unlike bombs they do not have tail vanes or attachments for them. These shells are dangerous if handled. They should be left alone and reported to the military authorities.

There may be special danger in the neighbourhood of wrecked aircraft, which has possibly unexploded missiles near it and bombs on board. The public are specially warned against collecting souvenirs. They may be dangerous and they may be wanted by the authorities for investigation. The safe rule is to leave things alone and report to the nearest warden or the police.

Above: Mrs E. Cullen is shown smiling as she emerges from the emergency exit at the back of her Anderson shelter. Debris from a bomb blast had blocked the main entrance. Published in *The Illustrated London News* this photograph is typical of a string of such images that demonstrated the almost indestructability of the shelters.

Left: A wartime cartoon. 'Is it all right now Henry?' 'Yes, not even scratched.'

CHAPTER 4

SHELTERS.

Heavy air attacks on this country have given an opportunity for a new and searching examination of shelter problems under the most realistic conditions. The Ministry of Home Security's shelter experts have used this opportunity to the utmost. They have made a constant study of the effects of air bombardment upon shelters of various kinds; and they have applied the lessons of the raids both to improve existing types and to devise new ones.

The raids have proved particularly the value of dispersal. It has been shown, too, that the walls of ordinary houses are a better protection against blast and splinters than was expected, and that such protection can be easily improved. These facts, added to the natural reluctance of most people to go night after night to distant public shelters, have led to the provision of many more small shelters which can be used in or near the home.

Types of Shelter.

Anderson Shelters.

The first of the official small shelters was the *Anderson*, which has been in use ever since the beginning of the raids and has done even greater things than was expected of it. It not only stands up well to blast and splinters, but because of its resilience it gives specially good protection against earth shock.

The Anderson should be erected in a yard or garden. Bunks to fit Anderson shelters are provided by the local authority, or can be made with a few feet of timber (2 in. by 2 in.) and some suitable lengths of canvas, hessian, or stout wire netting. The standard 6½ ft. Anderson shelter provides sleeping room for four adults and two small children (or four babies), and with extensions, any number up to twelve persons. Bunks for the adults should rest on the angle irons inside the shelter, and two smaller bunks (about 4½ ft by 2 ft., on legs about 14 ins. high) should be placed at the ends of the others. in such a way that the feet of the adults occupying the larger bunks pass under the smaller bunks.

Where flooding of an Anderson or other outdoor shelter is due to surface drainage water getting into the shelter, it can usually be cured by well ramming down the earth covering the top and sides, and by the construction of runnels in the ground outside to lead the water away to a drain or low ground well away from the shelter. If this does not keep out the water the earth covering should be removed, and the joints between the plates well sealed with strips of tarred rag or hessian and covered with clay-puddle made of a dough-like-mixture of ordinary clay and water. The earth should then be replaced in layers of 4 or 5 inches, each layer being well rammed or trodden down before the next is put on. The side slopes should be made even and well beaten down with a spade. There must be at least 18 ins. on top, and 30 ins. of earth at the sides, back and end of the shelter. If water still leaks through the joints on the inside of the shelter, they should be caulked on the inside with rope or old rags soaked in heavy oil or tar.

When the flooding is not serious but results from surface water finding its way through the shelter floor, a deep sump should be dug inside the shelter near the entrance and runnels sloping towards the sump should be dug across

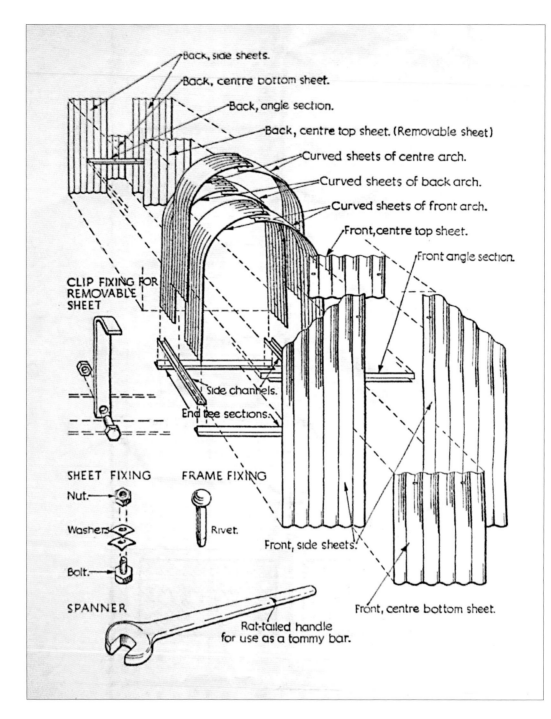

Back, side sheets.
Back, centre bottom sheet.
Back, angle section.
Back, centre top sheet. (Removable sheet)
Curved sheets of centre arch.
Curved sheets of back arch.
Curved sheets of front arch.
Front, centre top sheet.
Front angle section.

CLIP FIXING FOR
REMOVABLE
SHEET

Side channels.
End tee sections.

SHEET FIXING
Nut.
Washers
Bolt.

FRAME FIXING
Rivet.

Front, side sheets.

SPANNER
Rat-tailed handle
for use as a tommy bar.

Front, centre bottom sheet.

Above: Assembly instructions for the Anderson shelter. Consisting of only fourteen galvanised corrugated steel panels they were designed to be very simple to produce and to erect. The shelter was 6 feet high, 4 feet 6 inches long and 6 feet 6 inches wide, and in theory could accommodate up to six people. The internal fittings were left to the individual householder and most installed simple beds, although in the winter the shelters were cold and often suffered from damp or flooding. Extremely robust they nonetheless provided protection from blast and ground shock.

A completed Anderson Shelter.
(The baffle wall protecting the entrance is not visible in this photograph.)

the floor. The floor should then be covered with either a layer of bricks or a deep layer of clinker which may be smoothed off to form the floor, or over which a covering of linoleum or wood can be placed. Water can be baled out of the sump with small buckets or cans. The sump can best consist of a large tin or container perforated in its upper part, and provided with a suitable cover.

None of the foregoing methods will be successful if the flooding is due to the rise of subsoil water and the shelter floor lies below the sub-surface water level; but in such instances the flooding may possibly be cured by raising the level of the shelter floor, *e.g.*, by putting in a layer of earth covered with a layer of bricks or rubble or clinker. Another way is to raise the level of the shelter altogether; but if this is done, the shelter must be bedded in the earth not less than a foot, and the more it stands above ground level the more

'Why not be comfortable?' asked the *Picture Post* in October 1940. 'Long winter nights are ahead. With a little ingenuity you can make them tolerable by fitting your Anderson with home-made binks.'

The article featured the handiwork of Mr Stuart Murray in Croydon who, 'with a little ingenuity, had turned his shelter into a family bedroom. This was achieved by making bed frames out of 2x2-inch timber and covering them with chicken wire, taking care to fix a double layer in the centre where they are most likely to sag. The upper bunks were fitted with supports that rested on the shelter's steel girder. Packing-case boards were fixed at an angle to provide a substitute bolster on which to rest a pillow, and, finally, shelves were nailed between the bunks.

'Bedding, and any extra comforts you need imported from the house, will make the shelter more tolerable for an all-night session. It is not a difficult job. And, once done, it will mean a good deal to the health and the nerves of yourself and your family.'

Right: And so to bed. Mr and Mrs Murray enjoy the fruit of his labours. As the original article put it, 'Your timber and chicken wire framework, transformed with blankets and pillows, becomes, if not a bed of roses, a tolerable resting-place.'

earth must be packed round the sides and over the top. The local authority will give advice on such problems, and if the foregoing methods fail they may decide to line the shelter with concrete.

The condensation of moisture inside a steel shelter can be lessened by painting the inside of the ironwork with paint or shellac varnish and throwing some dry sawdust on to the paint while it is wet. Alternatively, the inside can be covered with linoleum, wall- or plaster-board, etc., fixed on wooden battens; or non-conducting material such as stout waterproof paper or absorbent material, such as felt may be fixed on wooden laths. Paper, such as ordinary wall-paper may be pasted directly on to the interior surface; this may not be so effective and will need renewing after a time, but is cheap.

Indoor Shelters.

The two chief types of shelter officially recommended for indoor use are the *Morrison* steel shelter and the timber framework type. Both are intended for use in ground floor or basement rooms of houses of two or at most three storeys. They must never be placed on the first or higher floors or in a ground floor room having a basement underneath. These shelters, while not proof against a direct hit, have been designed and constructed to withstand the much more likely risk of the upper part of the house collapsing on top of them. Both shelters have been tested thoroughly.

The Morrison shelter is 6 ft. 6 ins. long by 4 ft. wide, and will sleep two adults and one child, or two adults and two very small children. It consists of a strong frame, a flat top, a spring mattress forming a floor, and detachable sides of open mesh. The top is of sheet steel and has the advantage that it can be used as a table. The four steel mesh sides are made to resist blows from loose bricks and other debris, but can easily be opened from inside, providing four possible exits. The shelter is supplied in sections, with tools and simple instructions for putting it together. It should be placed, if possible, about 2 ft. away from a wall; or failing this, with one end against a wall—preferably a solid inside wall; but it should on no account be put right in a corner.

The Government makes a free distribution of Morrison shelters in selected areas, to people who have no other suitable shelter and whose annual income is not more than £350, plus certain allowances for children. A certain number of Morrison shelters are offered for sale, in certain areas, at £7 each. Application should be made to the local authority.

The timber framework type is built inside a room to take the weight of a top floor and roof falling in. The framework is almost ceiling high, so that it leaves the householder the normal use of practically the whole of the room. Timber for one framework costs about £4, to which must be added the cost of transport. The same amount of salvaged timber should cost from £1 to £3. The table has been designed by the Ministry of Home Security's shelter experts, and can be made at home by a handyman.

Full details about the timber table, the Morrison steel shelter and other forms of indoor shelter are given in a small illustrated government book called "*Shelter At Home.*" This book, a sequel to "Your Home as an Air-raid Shelter," is published at 3d. by H.M. Stationery Office, and is on sale throughout the country. It incorporates the most up-to-date expert advice on all problems of home shelter.

Commercially-made Indoor Shelters.

There are a number of these on the market. The Ministry of Home

The Morrison shelter
Officially termed Table (Morrison) Indoor Shelter, it was nothing more than a very strong cage, but, unlike the Anderson shelter, at least the Morrison shelter could be erected in the warmth and dry of the house. And, as these illustrations show, it could even double up as a dining table.

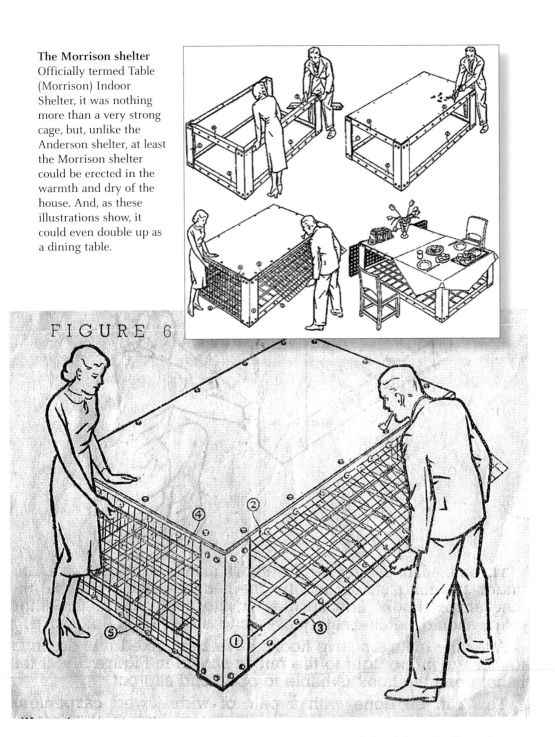

FIGURE 6

Above: Figure 6 from the instructions for erecting a Morrison shelter. 'The walls of most houses give good shelter from blast and splinters from a bomb falling nearby. The bomb, however, may also bring down part of the house, and additional protection from the fall of walls, floors and ceiling is therefore very essential. This is what the indoor shelter has been designed for.'

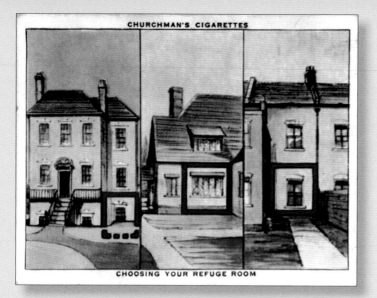

CHOOSING YOUR REFUGE ROOM

A refuge room

No. 1 in the Churchman series of Air Raid Precautions cards concerned the refuge room. The image above shows the rooms that should be chosen in typical houses for this role. A cellar or basement was best of all, provided that it was not subject to flooding, and had alternative means of exit. If you didn't have a cellar then the ground floor was the safest choise. The fewer external windows the better; and a room where the window was flanked by a building or strong wall was better than an exposed window. Having selected a room it was necessary to make it gas-proof and to install additional supports between the floor and the ceiling, either in the form of timber posts or scaffolding poles. Another card, below, illustrates some of the items you would need to equip the refuge room: Table and chairs. Gum and paper for sealing windows and cracks. Tinned food and a tin to contain bread, etc. Plates, cups, knives, forks, etc. Books, writing materials, cards, etc., to pass the time with. Wireless set, gramophone, etc. 'Heavy pieces of furniture should, if possible, be moved from the room immediately overhead.'

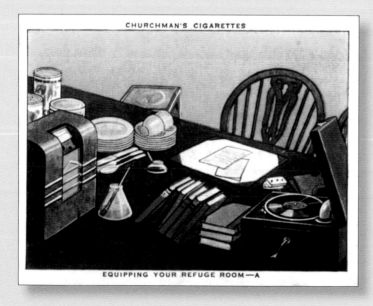

CHURCHMAN'S CIGARETTES

EQUIPPING YOUR REFUGE ROOM—A

Security provides facilities by which any manufacturer can have his shelter tested. Those shelters which have been tested and approved have the Ministry's certificate. Intending purchasers should not buy indoor shelters which have not secured this certificate.

Refuge Rooms.

Whether they have an indoor shelter or not, people who sleep at home in air raids should prepare at least one room in the house as a refuge room. " Shelter at Home " gives advice on the choice of a refuge room and the ways to protect it. A room facing the garden is generally better than one facing the street, because the soft earth will allow a bomb to go in deep before exploding, and so will reduce the danger from bomb splinters. The barricading of window openings with brick, concrete, or earth walls is a useful safety measure. If this is not done and the glass is left in the windows, it should receive some protective treatment. One of the best protections for window panes is a light-coloured cloth, such as cheese cloth, stuck to the inside of the window with flour paste ($\frac{1}{4}$ oz. of borax should be used to 1 pint of flour paste, to prevent mildew). Curtain net stuck on in the same way gives good protection; so does a screen of wire netting fixed on the inside of the window, provided the net has not a bigger mesh than $\frac{1}{2}$ in. If strips of sticky cloth tape are used, they should be criss-crossed so that no space of clear glass is more than 4 in. each way. Most of the lacquers and varnishes sold for strengthening glass need to be often renewed. Strips of ordinary paper give almost no protection.

To prevent the door of a refuge room from being blasted off, it is best to fasten it open, preferably with strong elastic round the handle. Heavy pieces of furniture should, if possible, be moved from the room immediately overhead.

Specialist Advice on Indoor Shelter.

The professional institutions of architects, engineers, and surveyors have appointed panels of consultants to inspect a private house at the request of the occupier and give a written report on the air raid protection arrangements which would be best suited to that house. The fee for this service is half a guinea. Most local authorities have lists of such consultants. If a local authority has no such list, application for the services of an approved consultant should be made to : The Secretary, Central Board of Advisory Panel of Professional Consultants, 1-7 Great George Street, Westminster, London, S.W.1.

Surface Shelters.

Large numbers of surface shelters have been built in the streets and open places, as well as in gardens where, for various reasons, the Anderson was unsuitable. Some surface shelters are to provide cover for any members of the public caught in the streets during raids. Others are allotted to particular families living near the shelters, and are used by them as dormitory shelters. Surface shelters allotted in this way are generally divided into compartments and shared among a group of neighbours, each family, or perhaps two or more families, having one section. Householders who are entitled and who wish to have the use of a surface shelter should apply to their local authority, who will install bunks and lighting and fit the shelter with a lock-up door. The key of the shelter is then kept by the people using it, and they are responsible for keeping the shelter clean and can do what they choose to make it comfortable.

The Second World War saw unprecedented numbers of people volunteering to play their part in defending Britain, turning members of the public into a new Home Front Army. These are the roof-spotters, scouring the sky for any sign of enemy aircraft. Their equipment is very simple, a pair of binoculars, a tin hat and two telephones with which to make urgent reports.

The surface shelter has the advantage of being usually near home, of giving greater comfort and privacy than is obtainable in a large public shelter, and at the same time of affording a very high degree of protection. The brick surface shelter was originally designed to stand up to splinters and blast from a 500-lb. bomb bursting a short distance away. Its performance in actual air raids has, in many instances, been even better than its designers anticipated; and the latest improvements in design give a still higher degree of protection.

Large Public Shelters.

Though the large public shelters can rarely provide the same rest and comfort as are obtainable at home or in smaller shelters, the conditions in public shelters show progressive improvement since heavy raiding began. Regular shelterers are now usually provided with bunks and entrance tickets so that queues and overcrowding are avoided. In very large shelters there is a sick bay with a trained nurse in attendance, and a doctor is readily available. Regular shelterers should make themselves familiar with these arrangements, and should give the shelter wardens and shelter committees all the co-operation they can.

People who are not clean, or who have an infectious disease, are not allowed to sleep in public shelters.

Practical Shelter Problems and How to Deal with Them.

Warmth in Shelters.

Inside small shelters, fires burning coal, coke, gas, or oil must not be used. They are very dangerous on account of the risk of poisoning from carbon-monoxide gas which cannot be smelt but which may lead to serious illness or death; they also use up some of the air and may be very dangerous if over-turned by a bomb explosion. One way to keep warm is by having a *hot drink*. This can be arranged even if you are sheltering away from home and have no vacuum flask. A bottle or tin will keep warm for a long time if thoroughly well packed in several layers of brown paper or newspaper or straw, and then wrapped round in a good thickness of blanket. An alternative is to make a " hay bottle." This is a woollen bag or loose woollen envelope large enough to take a bottle, with a loose lining which can be packed with newspaper or straw so as to retain as much of the heat from the bottle as possible. The bag with the bottle inside should be closely wrapped in a thick blanket or other warm material, or rolled up and securely tied inside a cloth bag.

Another way to keep warm in the shelter is to wear extra clothing, including perhaps a woollen helmet. A *sleeping bag* gives more warmth than any other kind of bed, and can be made very easily with two blankets. These should be placed one on the other, folded in half lengthwise and then sewn up along the bottom and open sides. Pieces of tape should be sewn at the open ends of the bag near the top and tied up when the owner is inside.

If only one blanket is available, it should be thickened for warmth. This is done very simply by lining it on one side with muslin or cotton material, stitching the lining to the blanket at intervals to form pockets and then stuffing the pockets with clean rags or pieces of newspaper. Finally, fold lengthwise and sew up. Paper will need changing at intervals, but it will keep out all draught and keep in the warmth generated by the body.

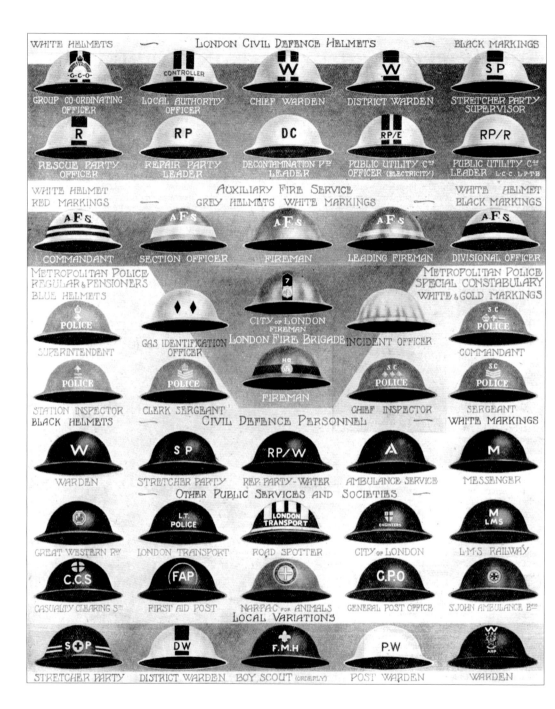

Above: Steel helmets of the Home Front in 1940. The various units of Britain's Civil Defence organisation had distinctive colourings and marking on their steel helmets to aid recognition. In the fourth row from the top it should be noted that the Gas Identification Officer's helmet was yellow with diamonds in black, while that of the Incident Officer had a light blue cloth cover tied over it.

WOMEN'S AUXILIARY
TERRITORIAL SERVICE

MECHANISED TRANSPORT
TRAINING CORPS

ENTERTAINMENTS
NATIONAL SERVICE
ASSOCIATION

FIRST AID NURSING
YEOMANRY

WOMEN'S AUXILIARY
AIR FORCE

NAVY, ARMY, & AIR
FORCE INSTITUTES

ROYAL NAVAL
PATROL SERVICE

WAR ORGANISATION OF
BRITISH RED CROSS SOCIETY
& ORDER OF St. JOHN

WOMEN'S LAND ARMY

AIR RAID PRECAUTIONS

METROPOLITAN
SPECIAL CONSTABULARY

CIVIL NURSING RESERVE

AUXILIARY
FIRE SERVICE

VOLUNTARY WORKERS
FOR THE FORCES

METROPOLITAN POLICE
WAR RESERVE

NATIONAL AIR
RAID PRECAUTIONS
ANIMALS COMMITTEE

MERCHANT NAVY

WOMEN'S VOLUNTARY
SERVICES

THE FRENCH
OF GREAT BRITAIN

WOMEN'S ROYAL
NAVAL SERVICE
(P.O. Badge)

BADGES OF AUXILIARY WAR SERVICES

Most of these badges need no description. The Mechanized Transport Training Corps was a voluntary organization of women transport drivers, etc. The R.N. Patrol Service had a minesweeping and an anti-submarine branch: the shark with its death-wound represents a U-boat. The A.R.P. badge gave place to one with the initials C.D. (Civil Defence), and when the Fire Service was nationalized its badge bore the letters N.F.S. Later, too, a shoulder flash superseded the Home Guard armlet.

A sleeping bag for a child can be made from pieces of blanket.

All sleeping bags should be thoroughly ironed inside and out at least once a month.

People sleeping without a mattress, whether on bunks or anywhere else, should be protected underneath with a good layer of blankets, newspapers or thick brown paper. A *hot brick* will keep a bed warm. It should be heated in front of a fire for about two hours, then wrapped in a woollen cloth or old vest and put in the bed.

A simple *flower-pot heater*, useful in a small shelter, can be made by placing a flower-pot on a couple of bricks to raise it from the ground, fixing a lighted candle by the drain-hole at the bottom of the flower-pot (without, however, blocking up the hole) and then turning a second flower-pot upside-down on top of the first flower-pot, edge to edge. After a time the top flower-pot will give off considerable warmth.

The coal-burning stove, used in some public shelters, is safe, provided that the right precautions are taken over screening, ventilation, stoking, and regular cleaning of the flue-pipes.

Any coal stove in use in a public shelter should on no account be interfered with by the shelterers. They should not use it for cooking or for warming drinks without the warden's permission. The wire guard round it should not be removed.

It is worth remembering that when there are a number of people in a shelter the temperature soon rises because of the warmth given off by their bodies, and that therefore even without heating arrangements a shelter that seems cold at first may seem very warm after a few hours. Shelterers should have extra clothing to put on, to avoid getting a chill if they go out of the shelter into the open.

Curtains at entrances and round bunks will help to keep out draughts.

Lighting of Shelters.

If possible, a shelter should be lighted by electricity. Gas and oil lights should be avoided. Naked lights have the disadvantage that they use up fresh air and introduce a risk of fire; but candles may be used if there is no electricity. Alternative lighting, such as candles, a lantern or a torch, should always be provided in case the electricity supply should fail.

Ventilation in Shelters.

An outside shelter may be ventilated by an outlet pipe or vent hole which should be placed at the end of the shelter as far away from the entrance and as near the roof as possible. To keep in the light and keep out the rain, the top of a vent pipe should be covered with a cowl or T-piece or angle-piece, and for covering up a vent hole a movable piece of sheet iron should be provided.

A shelter should always be kept as empty as possible of unessential articles such as ornaments. The less the people in a shelter move about, the less of the available air they will use up.

After a shelter has been occupied, it should be given a thorough airing.

Shelter Health and Comfort Hints.

(1) If you take your children out to shelter at night, dress them in night-wear under their other clothing.

(2) If you go out to shelter, take stockings and slippers, so you can change if your feet get wet.

(3) Give your bedding a thorough airing every day, and see that it is always clean. If you take bedding to a public shelter, carry it in a large soft bag or haversack, rather than in a hard basket or case that will take up valuable space.

(4) If you take a baby to a shelter, take also toilet paper, spare napkins, and a rubber bag for soiled napkins.

(5) Keep the shelter free from litter and scraps.

(6) Wear clean clothes in the shelter, wash thoroughly before and after sleeping in the shelter, and gargle as often as you can. A teaspoonful of salt in half a pint of water makes a good gargle, and should be sniffed up the nostrils as well.

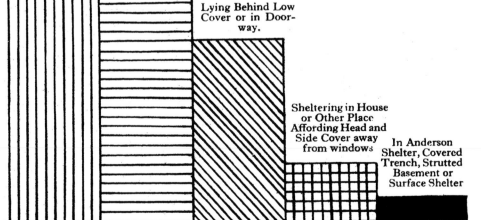

This diagram is based on a large number of reports of the results of recent air raids, and is an approximate indication of the difference in the degree of risk resulting from taking cover in various ways.

47

(7) Remember that children and people going to work need to get to sleep early.

(8) When you go to shelter, take your gasmask, identity card and ration book, record of insurance or instalment payments and other important papers.

Animals and Shelters.

Animals are not allowed in public shelters. They can be taken to an animals' shelter (marked with the sign : N.A.R.P.A.C.). If taken into a private shelter or refuge room, they should if possible be kept in the basket or kennel to which they are accustomed. A dog should be kept on a lead, and preferably muzzled. Sedative pills for animals may be obtained from a chemist, veterinary surgeon or animal guard. Cats and dogs found straying after air raids are cared for at animal detention posts, run by animal guards; and if the animal is wearing an identity disc, its owner can usually be found. This disc is obtainable from the local animal guard, whose address can be supplied by the warden, or by the National A.R.P. Animals' Committee, 2, West Heath Avenue, London, N.W.11.

SEE THAT YOUR WARDEN KNOWS WHERE YOU AND YOUR FAMILY ARE TAKING SHELTER

CHAPTER 5

WAR GASES.

I. The Nature of Gas Attacks.

The word " gas " as used in war means any chemical substance, whether solid, liquid, or vapour, employed to produce poisonous or irritant effects upon the human body. A war gas may be used by itself, or it may be used in combination with other gases so as to make the identification of any one of them more difficult.

The strength or proportion of gas in the air at any one place is referred to as the gas " *concentration* " : and the higher the concentration (i.e. the stronger the mixture) the greater will be the harmful or harassing effect of the gas.

The pollution of any object by war gas is called " *contamination*," and " *decontamination* " means, in this connection, the cleansing of anyone or anything from war gas.

There are two categories of poison gases : non-persistent and persistent; both may be dropped in bombs, and persistent gas also in other containers, or sprayed.

Non-persistent gases are so called because however they are released they are almost instantly converted into gas or smoke which drifts along with the wind and gradually becomes less effective as it mixes with larger quantities of air. Non-persistent gases, therefore, are ordinarily effective only for a short time, though in still weather or where the air movement is restricted by buildings, the process of dispersal and dilution is slower. The bursting of a bomb of non-persistent gas would produce a dangerous concentration of gas which would probably not last for more than 20 minutes at any one spot, though the incident would affect an area for some distance down-wind from the point of burst.

Persistent gases are released usually in liquid form, and are called persistent because they evaporate slowly and give off dangerous vapour for a long time. In warm weather the evaporation is faster and the vapour, therefore, more harmful. In very cold weather the liquid freezes and gives off no vapour. In its frozen state it is safe if left alone. The liquid is always dangerous to touch and wherever it falls, even if only in small drops or splashes, it contaminates everything with which it comes into contact. Unless it is removed or neutralised, it continues to give off dangerous vapour until completely evaporated. The vapour, like a non-persistent gas, is eventually dissipated into the air; and this process is slower in a built-up area than in open country, where the air moves more freely.

If persistent gas is dropped in a bomb the area where the bomb bursts becomes splashed with liquid gas and has to be decontaminated. Anyone near is likely to be splashed with the liquid or to be affected by the poisonous vapour coming from it. If the gas is sprayed instead of dropped in a bomb the effects are likely to be more widespread but less dangerous, because the gas concentration in any one place will be less.

Heavy rain tends to wash any gas out of the air and to wash away concentrations of liquid gas from exposed surfaces. Non-persistent gases are

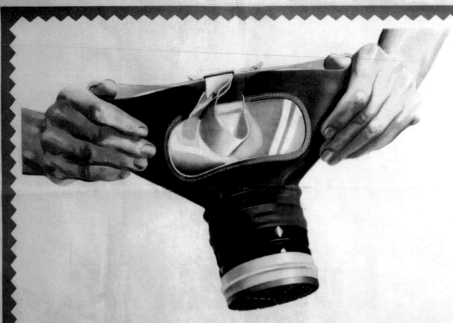

Hitler will send no warning –

so always carry your gas mask

ISSUED BY THE MINISTRY OF HOME SECURITY

50

most dangerous in dry, calm weather, when their dispersal is slow. Persistent gases are most dangerous in dry weather, when there is a high ground temperature to intensify evaporation and a light breeze to spread the dangerous vapour.

Non-persistent gases are normally invisible, except in very high concentration. Persistent gases are, of course, visible in liquid form, but the vapour given off by the liquid is invisible. Besides the Gas Identification Services, both wardens and police are fully trained to recognise the symptoms of a gas attack and to give the public warning and advice. A description of the smells of various gases is given in the " Table of War Gases," on page 62, but this should be taken only as a rough guide, since the smells of gases might easily be camouflaged or altered.

II. General Protective Measures Against Gas.

When the gas-rattles give warning of a gas attack the first thing everyone should do is to put on his gas-mask at once, and keep it on until the hand-bells sound the " gas clear." It has been proved by continual experiment that the ordinary civilian mask gives full protection against any known war-gas to the eyes, nose, throat or lungs; and that provided the gas-mask is properly cared for it retains its protective properties almost indefinitely. Instructions on the use and care of gas-masks are given on pages 36-43. People who follow these simple instructions, and who in addition remember to have their gas-masks always by them, are assured of the best possible safeguard against the risks stated above.

Out of doors in a gas attack it must be borne in mind that if there is any wind the areas affected by the gas will be down-wind from where the gas has fallen. Anyone wanting to get away from the effects of a concentration of gas should, therefore, go diagonally up-wind, moving, of course, to one side to avoid the point where the gas was released and where the concentration will be greatest.

During a gas attack everyone who can do so should put on his respirator and get under cover as quickly as possible. People indoors who see others caught in the street in a gas attack will no doubt offer them shelter. Inside any building, provided the doors and windows are shut, there is less likelihood of a strong concentration of gas than outside, and less risk of being contaminated by liquid gas. But clothing contaminated by blister gas must be removed before the wearer goes indoors. People who have to be out should have their coat-collars up and their sleeves pulled down over their wrists and do their best to keep the whole of themselves well covered, remembering that though the gas-mask gives protection to the face and lungs, the danger with liquid gas is that it will blister any part of the skin exposed to it (see p. 33) and, therefore, the whole body needs to be well covered up if the presence of liquid gas is suspected. If the occupants of a damaged house should have to leave home during a gas attack and find other shelter, they should keep on their gas-masks and if possible wear mackintoshes and gum-boots.

All doors and windows should be closed. It is true that upstairs rooms are safer from gas than downstairs ones, because all the likely war gases are heavier than air and, therefore, stay near the ground and remain longest in low-lying places; but as high explosives may be expected with gas attacks, it would probably be best to rely on one's gas mask for protection against gas and stay low down in the building for safety from high explosives. One gas-proof room in a house is certainly an asset, and instructions for making such a room are given on page 45; but under raid conditions a gas-proof

THE CIVILIAN RESPIRATOR

Civilian Respirators

Top left: This consisted of a face-piece, to which was attached by means of a rubber band a cylindrical metal container containing the filters. The face-piece was held in position by means of webbing straps that fitted around the head. These came in three sizes and were issued to the public free of charge. (Lost respirators were also replaced free of charge.) They came in a protective cardboard box and were to be carried at all times.

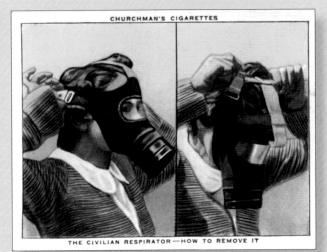

THE CIVILIAN RESPIRATOR—HOW TO REMOVE IT

Left: There was a right way to remove the respirator, as shown here. This was done by slipping the head harness forward from the back of the head. It was important to do this correctly, as taking the gas mask off by pulling on the container risked cracking the transparent plastic window. As can be seen opposite, the Civilian Duty Respirators had more substantial glazed eye pieces.

Right: Home Office mobile gas vans were used for the testing of respirators and for training under the conditions of a gas attack. The white canopies at the back are airlocks to stop the gas escaping when the door of the van is opened. The picture shows a group of trainees at the Hendon Police College in London.

MOBILE GAS VANS

Civilian Duty Respirators

Top right: Air Raid Wardens were volunteers enrolled by the local authorities. The card shows wardens handing reports to a volunteer despatch-rider. All are wearing steel helmets and Civilian Duty Respirators. The wardens are also wearing identification armlets over their civilian clothes. Note the shading device on the motorcycle's headlamp.

Right: The Civilian Duty Respirator was of stronger construction than the civilian version and was intended for those who might have to work in the presence of gas. The face-piece was of moulded rubber and the eye pieces were of strong glass. There was an outlet valve above the nose, and a small cylinder on the side of the mask accommodated a microphone for speaking on the telephone.

CHURCHMAN'S CIGARETTES

AIR RAID WARDENS AND CIVILIAN VOLUNTEER DESPATCH-RIDER

CHURCHMAN'S CIGARETTES

THE CIVILIAN DUTY RESPIRATOR

CHURCHMAN'S CIGARETTES

A HEAVY ANTI-GAS SUIT

Left: A heavy anti-gas suit as used by members of a Decontamination Squad. It consisted of an oilskin suit, rubber boots and gloves, and respirator. A hood was also worn, although not shown in this picture. The suit provided complete protection against liquid or vapour of mustard gas.

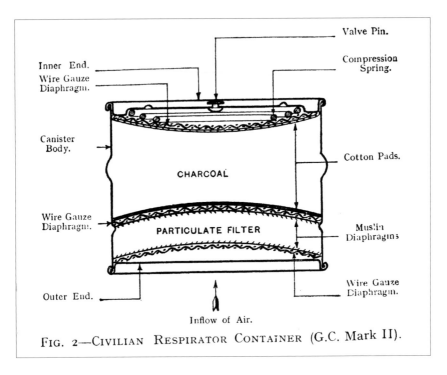

FIG. 2—CIVILIAN RESPIRATOR CONTAINER (G.C. Mark II).

Diagrams showing gas mask containers. The one for the basic Civilian Respirator (G.C. Mark II) is shown above, and the Service Respirator (Training Type A), below.

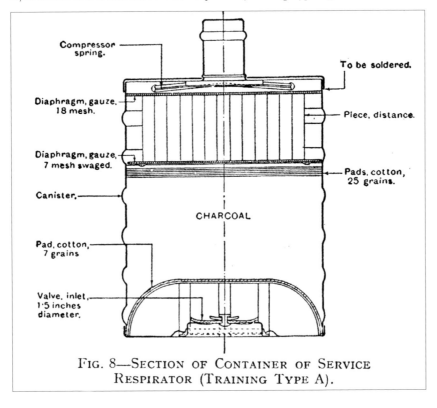

FIG. 8—SECTION OF CONTAINER OF SERVICE RESPIRATOR (TRAINING TYPE A).

Given the devastating use of poisonous gas in the First World War, initially by Germany in early 1915, but later by both sides, there was a very genuine fear in the lead-up to the Second World War that gas might be used again, this time against the civilian population. Extensive precautions were taken including the issuing of gas masks and training in how to use them in all manner of situations.

Top: Members of the London Transport staff practise relaying railway track in full gas protection suits.

Middle right: Female members of the Auxiliary Fire Service receive instruction in the use of gas masks.

Bottom right: Wandsworth ARP wardens in training wearing protective gear. Note the rattle to give a gas warning. A whistle would have been completely useless if you were wearing a gas mask.

WANDSWORTH A.R.P.
GAS DETECTION

WANDSWORTH A.R.P.
AIR RAID WARDENS

room could easily be damaged, especially by blast. Therefore, even in a gas-proof room, everyone should have his gas mask handy.

When the "gas clear" is sounded, all doors and windows should be thrown open to clear the air. This can be speeded up by lighting fires to create draughts, and by using large sheets of cardboard to fan the air towards open doors and windows.

III. Effects of Particular Gases, and How to Deal with Them.

War gases may be classified, according to their effects on the body, into two categories : *non-blister* and *blister*. Important non-blister gases are : lung irritants, eye irritants, and nose irritants.

Lung irritants (choking gases) of which phosgene is the most deadly, are usually non-persistent gases. In strong concentrations they immediately produce smarting and watering of the eyes, irritation of the throat and violent coughing and retching (this is specially marked with chlorine and chloropicrin). Strong concentrations of these gases, even if breathed only for a short time, may cause death.

Anyone who has been exposed without a gas-mask to a lung-irritant gas must be spared further exertion, whether he shows symptoms of injury or not. He must be kept lying down and protected from chill, and he should be removed to hospital as a stretcher case.

Eye irritants (tear gases) may be either persistent or non-persistent. Even in low concentrations they cause extreme smarting and watering of the eyes. The effects are only temporary, and soon pass off if the victim leaves the affected area or puts on his gas-mask. Tear gases are effective as harassing agents and might be used to cause panic and threaten morale. In liquid form these gases resemble blister gas, and they might be used with blister gas to mask its presence.

Nose irritants (sneezing gases) are non-persistent, and consist of very fine particles of solid arsenical compounds liberated in the form of a dust or smoke, generally visible and with practically no smell. Nose gases produce intense irritation and pain in the nose, mouth, throat and chest, and very often cause sneezing and headaches.

These effects, which may not appear until a few moments after exposure, are sometimes accompanied by acute mental distress. When the victim puts on his gas-mask, relief will probably not come at once, so that he thinks the gas-mask is no good and this, combined with the nauseating effect of the gas, may make him inclined to take the gas-mask off again. He must on no account do this, especially as a nose gas might be used at the same time as a more deadly gas. The effects of nose irritants will normally pass off quickly if the gas-mask is put on promptly and kept on until the gas attack is over.

A nose gas is most unlikely to cause permanent injury. Anyone suffering from vomiting during an attack of nose gas should not remove the face-piece of the gas-mask but should bend forward, turn the head to one side, raise the corner of the face-piece at the angle of the jaw while vomiting and drop the face-piece back into place between expulsive spasms. It is important that the face-piece should fall back into place immediately, before the involuntary intake of breath that follows the vomiting spasm.

Blister Gases.

Contamination by these gases is particularly insidious and can have far-reaching effects. Blister gases in both liquid and vapour form are readily absorbed by all porous substances, and these, once contaminated, continue to give off poisonous vapour and to be dangerous to touch even after all

56

visible signs of the contamination have disappeared. The contamination may be spread by anyone touching a contaminated surface, and by animals and vehicles.

The effect of these gases whether in liquid or vapour form is to burn and blister skin. Clothes give some protection for a time but a sufficient concentration of blister gas can penetrate ordinary clothing, and may, therefore, cause serious injuries to any part of the body. Internal injury may result from breathing in large quantities of the vapour, or from eating food that has been contaminated by either the liquid or the vapour. Prolonged exposure to the vapour injures the eyes, and if the liquid gets into the eyes it may cause blindness. Short exposure to a low concentration of blister-gas vapour has normally no ill effects.

The two most important blister gases are lewisite and mustard gas. Both are liquids that give off invisible vapour.

Lewisite, in the impure form used in war, is immediately recognisable by its strong smell of geraniums. In vapour form this gas at once irritates the eyes and nose. In liquid form, even in tiny drops, it makes the skin tingle.

Mustard gas can be far more treacherous, because it sometimes is much more difficult to detect. It has an indefinite smell (some people liken it to onions, others to mustard) and as the gas is breathed the smell becomes less distinguishable. At the same time neither the liquid nor the vapour seems to produce any immediately noticeable injury, unless the liquid happens to get into the eyes and makes them sting. It is, therefore, possible to be exposed to mustard gas without knowing it until serious harm has been done.

Decontamination of People Exposed to Blister Gas.

After exposure to blister gas the success of the treatment depends on the speed with which it is applied.

Anyone who has been exposed to the liquid must go at once to the nearest place (whether his own or someone else's house, or a public cleansing station) where he can take off his clothes and wash thoroughly all over in soap and water, preferably warm. Similar precautions should be taken by anyone who has been exposed for some time to vapour. Simple facilities are sufficient for cleansing and it is important that people should be ready to cleanse themselves, and to admit passers-by into their homes for cleansing purposes. Contaminated clothing and footwear must be left outside the building, to avoid contaminating other people. It is especially important not to carry contamination into crowded places such as public shelters.

Splashes of liquid blister gas on the skin must be dealt with immediately. If large drops are visible it is best to swab them off at once with a rag or series of rags, taking care not to spread the gas further on the skin. Rags that have been used for removing gas are dangerous and should be burnt or disposed of so that they do not infect anyone else. A receptacle for these contaminated swabs will be found outside chemists' shops. If no rag is available for removing the gas no time should be wasted looking for one.

Any part of the skin contaminated by liquid blister gas should have *anti-gas ointment No.* 2 applied to it at once and according to the directions on the jar. This ointment is obtainable at any chemist's. When there is no anti-gas ointment No. 2 available, *bleach cream* should be used. It should be rubbed on to the affected part for one minute, left on for another minute and then wiped off. If the face is treated with bleach cream, care must be taken not to get it in the eyes. When blister gas is used in a raid there will be pails of bleach cream outside the doors of chemists' shops, together with a poster giving full directions.

If neither anti-gas ointment No. 2 nor bleach cream is immediately available, the contaminated part of the skin should be scrubbed thoroughly with soap and water.

(*Note.*—Bleach paste and anti-gas ointment are harmful to textile materials, and therefore must not get into contact with clothes, or fabric articles such as respirator haversacks. The outsides of all tins and pots containing the paste or ointment must be cleaned after use, and hands smeared with the paste or ointment should not touch clothes or other materials. Fabrics accidentally affected should be washed thoroughly, if possible after being swabbed with a 5 per cent. solution of photographic hypo.)

If the eyes have been exposed to blister gas, whether vapour or liquid, they should at once be washed thoroughly with warm water or with a weak solution of salt or bicarbonate of soda (about one teaspoonful of salt or bicarbonate of soda to a pint of water). If there is no apparatus for eye-douching, one of the following improvised measures should be adopted :

(i) The casualty should bend over a bowl containing warm water or one of the mild fluids referred to above, and put the eyes, each in turn, well under water. They should be opened under water and the head moved from side to side. If one eye is unaffected, it must be kept out of the contaminated fluid until the affected eye has been cleansed, after which both eyes should be douched in a fresh solution.

(ii) The eyes should be opened in turn under a gentle stream of water (e.g. from a tap, from a rubber or other tube attached to a tap, or from a kettle or teapot), the head being moved slightly from side to side, and each eye opened and closed from time to time. Care must be taken that the wash water from a contaminated eye does not enter an unaffected one.

People who are seriously injured as well as contaminated should be given essential first-aid and eye or skin treatment on the spot, if that is possible, and then be removed direct to hospital by stretcher and ambulance.

Wardens, police, and first-aiders may be able to deal on the spot with people who are slightly injured and also contaminated. If not, such people must go immediately to the nearest first-aid post or hospital, where they will receive cleansing treatment as well as the necessary first aid.

Signs of injury from blister gas may not be evident for some hours after decontamination. Anyone affected in this way should report at once to the nearest hospital or first-aid post.

Decontamination of Clothes.

Badly contaminated clothes which have been exposed to blister gas vapour will show dark stains and should be put in a dustbin with a close-fitting lid and left outside the house, to be collected for decontamination by the local authority.

Clothes exposed to vapour and less badly contaminated should be hung in the open air for at least 24 hours. If then they still smell of gas, they should be left for collection as described above.

Light dresses and underclothing, if only slightly contaminated by vapour, should be aired and then washed for at least 15 minutes with soap and warm water.

Clothes contaminated by liquid blister gas, or suspected of being so, should not be decontaminated at home, nor in fact taken into any building. They should be left for collection in a dustbin as described above. Decontamination does not normally injure clothes.

Decontamination of Leather Footwear.

This is a difficult matter, and, therefore, great care should be taken to avoid stepping into splashes of liquid gas.

Before going indoors, people who have walked through contaminated areas should examine the soles and uppers of their boots for signs of contamination, taking care not to infect the hands. If there is any smear or smell of blister gas the boots must be put somewhere out of doors, where they will not infect anyone, and must be left for collection by the local decontamination squad. It would be a wise precaution in any case to take the boots off before entering the house and air them outside for 24 hours.

IV. Food and Poison Gas.

Food exposed to poison gas may be rendered unfit to eat. Therefore, if gas attacks develop, people in vulnerable areas should protect food by keeping it in airtight wrappers, tins, or bottles, and should avoid drinking liquid unless it comes direct from a tap or out of a covered container.

Wrappers should be of waxed or greaseproof paper. Food containers of wood or cardboard readily absorb liquid gas, and so these should be covered with waxed or greaseproof paper. Larders should be kept closed. A refrigerator provides excellent gas-proof storage.

Food contaminated by liquid gas must at once be reported to the local A.R.P. authority, who will arrange for its disposal. Food thought to be contaminated should be left alone until the local A.R.P. authority has been consulted. Food in contaminated air-tight tins or bottles may be safe if the containers can be decontaminated, but it should not be touched until it has been approved by the local A.R.P. authority.

V. How to Use and Look After Your Gas Mask.

Everyone in the country is entitled to a Government respirator. All respirators issued by the Government remain Government property. They are for use against war gases and do not give protection against domestic coal gas or other noxious gases.

The three chief types of civilian respirators are the general civilian gas mask, the small child's gas mask for children aged from about 18 months to 4 years, and the baby's anti-gas helmet for babies in arms.

Special respirators are available for people who on account of breathing difficulties, tracheotomy, facial deformity, or severe heart trouble, are unable to wear the ordinary type. A special respirator requires a doctor's certificate.

The General Civilian Gas Mask.

This gas mask has a window of non-inflammable transparent material let into a face-piece of thin sheet rubber which covers the eyes, nose, and mouth, and which is held in position by head harness. A container attached to the face-piece holds activated charcoal to absorb poison gas from the incoming air, and a filter to prevent the passage of fine particles of poisonous smoke.

Most civilian gas masks have an additional filter, known as " Contex," attached by adhesive tape. This filter improves the protective qualities of the mask. More recently issued gas masks are fully effective without " Contex." These masks are marked with a green band.

Air is breathed in through the container and is prevented from passing back through the same channel by a simple non-return valve consisting of a flat rubber disc attached to the inner end of the container. As air is breathed out it forces its way between the edges of the rubber facepiece and the cheeks, so that a separate outlet is unnecessary.

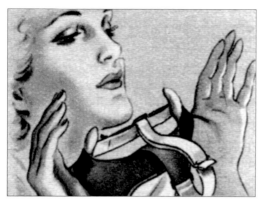

Putting on gas mask.   First position.

At night, masks on; close windows without showing light.

Gas alert while in the street.

Having put on masks take cover.

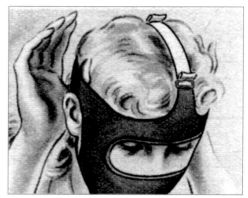

With straps drawn over head.

The facepiece of the gas mask is provided in three standard sizes: small, medium and large. An extra large size is now available for exceptionally large faces. The size is marked on the headstraps or moulded on the brow of the facepiece. The same container is fitted to all types.

The small size of civilian gas mask will fit most children from 4 years upwards as well as some exceptionally developed children under 4 years.

Putting on the gas mask should be a matter of seconds. After a gas alarm the first thing to do is to hold the breath, as it may be dangerous to breathe in before the gas mask is in place.   Hat and spectacles or pince-nez must be taken off before the mask is put on, otherwise they may interfere with the fit. Women should see that there are no hairpins to get in the way, and that the hair is pushed back so that it will not get under the facepiece.

The gas mask should be held in front of the face by each of the side straps, with the thumbs under the straps.   The chin should be thrust into the facepiece, and the straps drawn over the head as far as they will reach comfortably. The next thing is to breathe out violently to expel any gas that may have got inside the facepiece; after which normal breathing can be resumed.   The hat can then be put on, over the headstraps.

A properly-adjusted gas mask shows the buckle in the centre at the crown of the head, and the facepiece straight on the face with the two side straps horizontal. It is important not to have the edges of the facepiece doubled under, or the straps twisted.

When once the head-straps have been adjusted correctly they should be left fastened in the right position with safety-pins, and the position of the buckle on the straps should be marked with a lead pencil. As children grow adjustments are necessary from time to time to make sure that the mask remains comfortable and fits properly.

A correctly-adjusted gas mask should be quite comfortable, and provide a gastight fit in all positions of the head.

A correctly-fitting gas mask shows the eyes on a line about midway between the upper and lower edges of the transparent window panel. If the eyes are much below this line the gas mask is too large; if they are much above, the mask is too small.

When the fit is too loose the air breathed in may not pass through the purifying materials in the container. This can be tested by holding a piece of very thin paper against the outer end of the "Contex" (or a piece of flat cardboard against the end of a container without "Contex") and then trying to breathe in. If it is impossible to breathe in and the facepiece is sucked in against the cheeks, the fit is gastight.

When the rubber facepiece is stretched too tightly it will be uncomfortable because of the pressure on the face and the undue resistance to the exhaled air which must pass between the facepiece and the cheeks. Any resistance to breathing will be found most exhausting and must be remedied either by adjusting the head-harness or getting a larger gas mask.

To take off a gas mask the thumb of the right hand should be put under the buckle at the back of the head and the straps drawn forward over the top of the head and then down, the left hand meanwhile supporting the weight of the container.

Any other method of taking off a gas mask may damage the facepiece.

It is essential to have regular practice in putting on, wearing and taking off the gas mask, both in daylight and dark.

The Small Child's Gas Mask.

Children sometimes do not take kindly to wearing gas masks; but the Small Child's Gas Mask has been designed to make it as acceptable as possible. The colours are attractive; the mask is as light as possible; the head-harness is gentle in its pull on the facepiece but all the same will stand considerable usage and prevents the mask from being easily pulled off. As a child breathes less air than an adult the container, which is screwed into the facepiece, is less bulky and lighter than that of the ordinary civilian gas mask.

The container offers only a negligible resistance to the child's breathing, and exhaled air passes out of the facepiece by a soft rubber valve which opens freely under pressure of the breath. When " Contex " is attached, it is joined to the end of the container by means of a close-fitting adhesive band.

The facepiece, which is fitted with two glass eye-pieces, is made of soft rubber which readily takes the shape of the child's face and makes close contact with the skin.

The Small Child's Gas Mask is put on in the same way as the ordinary civilian type. Many children soon learn to put on the mask for themselves if they are shown how to thrust the chin forward into it. When someone else puts the gas mask on the child, he should do so from behind, with the back of the child's head resting against his chest, so that the child's neck is supported against the action of pulling the elastic harness over the head. *All children should practise wearing their gas masks regularly.*

To remove the Small Child's Gas Mask, the head-harness at the back of the head must be unhooked and drawn downwards off the face with the right hand whilst the left hand supports the container.

Adjustment of the head-harness is automatic. When the respirator is properly put on with the harness secured by means of the hook and eye at the back, the fit of the respirator is automatically ensured if the child's face is not too large or too small and it can easily be seen if there is the necessary close contact between the rubber and the face.

There is only one size of Small Child's Respirator. If there is difficulty in stretching the head-harness over the head, or if the eyes are unduly high in the eyepieces, this type of respirator is too small for the child, and a small civilian type should be used. If the facepiece of the Small Child's Respirator puckers at the edges or is loose on the face, or if the eyes are unduly low in the eyepieces, the child is too small for this type, and the Baby's Anti-Gas Protective Helmet should be used.

The Baby's Protective Helmet.

This helmet is designed for infants in arms up to the age of about 18 months, and young children who show a marked objection to the Small Child's Respirator, or are otherwise temperamentally or physically unfitted to wear it.

The Baby's Helmet consists of a hood made of impervious fabric and fitted with a large window which encloses the child's head, shoulders, and arms, and is closed around the child's waist by means of a draw tape. A baby inside the helmet is, therefore, able to get its hand to its mouth. The hood is surrounded by and fastened to a light metal frame, which is lengthened on the underside and fitted with a tailpiece so as to form a support and protection for the baby's back. The metal frame may be varied in length to suit all sizes of babies and children up to about 5 years of age, and the length should be such that the baby's face is opposite the middle of the window. The tailpiece can be made extra long, if required, by overlapping the movable sections on the last two screw-holes only and using an extra screw and nut in the hole which has no fixed nut. A spare screw and nut for this purpose will be found on the domed top of the frame.

The tailpiece is turned up at the end to form a seat which prevents the child from slipping out of the hood, and the child is further secured in the helmet by means of a T-shaped supporting strap connected to the end of the tailpiece, and fastened on each side of the child to metal buckles in the frame.

The hood is padded on the underside where the baby rests, but padding has been omitted from the tailpiece, as babies are likely to soil any padding in this position. Mothers can, if they like, supply some washable padding, such as a folded towel or napkin, for this part of the frame.

Folding legs are provided on the metal frame to prevent the helmet from rolling over if it is laid down, for instance, when the baby is being put into it.

Air is supplied to the inside of the hood by means of rubber bellows, best operated by the right hand. The air passes through a container (fitted with " Contex "), which removes all poison gas and it enters the hood at the top through a specially shaped orifice, which deflects the air upwards so that it sweeps out all vitiated air from the hood and also prevents the stream of air from blowing directly on the baby's head.

After about twelve quick strokes to clear the stale air out of the helmet, a slow and steady rate of pumping of about forty strokes a minute should be maintained. This will be adequate for keeping out gas and supplying enough purified air even for a child of four to five years of age. The space in the hood is large enough to allow pumping to be stopped for several minutes without causing discomfort to the child. When pumping, the operator should use the fingers only and not the palm of the hand, so as not to obstruct the intake holes which lie in the disc at the movable end of the bellows.

There is no limit to the time during which a child may remain in the helmet if steady pumping is maintained.

The helmet should never be taken to pieces by an unskilled person, because there is a risk of its being reassembled wrongly.

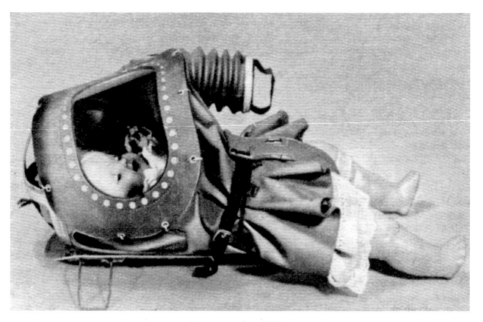

Baby's Anti-Gas Helmet.

How to Put the Baby into the Helmet.

(1) The wire legs of the helmet should be opened and clipped back.

(2) The helmet should be laid down with the skirt of the bag open and the top turned back over the window. The wide strap attached to the turned-up end of the metal tailpiece should be placed out of the way, so that the baby will not lie upon it.

(3) The baby should be placed in the helmet so that its seat rests in the curve of the tailpiece with one leg on each side.

(4) The skirt should then be pulled down over the baby and both the baby's arms should be free and put up inside the bag before the tape is tied. The ends should then be drawn snugly, but not too tightly, around the baby's waist, and tied in a bow that can be quickly and easily undone.

(5) The wide supporting strap should now be brought up between the legs and the ends of the canvas straps attached to the buckles on each side of the frame so as to hold the baby firmly in place. If the frame is being used in one of its shorter positions, it may be necessary to shorten the

wide supporting strap so that it will hold the child securely. This may be done by folding down the top end, either once or twice, as required. and passing the ends of the canvas strap out through the metal slots.

(6) When the baby has thus been safely fastened in the helmet, the bellows should be operated. (See above.)

The baby in the helmet, with the legs folded, can be nursed on the lap or carried in the arms in the normal way. If the baby has to be carried some distance, a wide shawl should be used as a sling to support the helmet from the mother's shoulders.

It is essential that parents should practise fitting and operating the helmet both in daylight and in darkness, and when wearing a respirator.

As the child grows, the length of the helmet must be adjusted so that the child will be comfortable and fully protected.

The carton in which the baby's helmet is supplied is only large enough, with the normal method of packing, to take the helmet with the tailpiece unextended, but if the tailpiece has had to be extended to fit the child, it should always be kept extended so that the helmet can be put on quickly in an emergency. At the same time, it is important not to tear the carton, as cardboard is scarce. Therefore, when the tailpiece is extended, the carton should be packed as follows :

The flap of one end of the carton should be turned down inside the carton and the helmet inserted upside down in the carton, with the extended tailpiece sticking out over the end of the turned-down flap. The other end-flap and the side-flaps should then be closed over the top and a piece of string tied round to keep the flaps down. Except for the projecting tailpiece, the carton will then enclose the whole helmet and keep it reasonably free from light and dust.

(Wardens will demonstrate this method if required.)

Inspection of Gas Masks.

From time to time a civilian gas mask should be taken out of its case and set aside for a while so that the face-piece can " loosen up," otherwise it may get distorted.

All gas masks should be inspected regularly, preferably by a warden. Uninstructed people should not tamper with the delicate sections.

The transparent window piece is the part most easily damaged, and the gas mask must never be folded in a way to kink or bend this section. Cracks or weaknesses in the window piece can be seen by holding it in front of the light. A damaged eye panel should be replaced as soon as possible through the local warden or A.R.P. office. In an emergency the panel can be made gastight by applying adhesive tape (transparent if possible) over the split on both surfaces.

The stitching round the edges of the window piece should be secure. The thin rubber of the facepiece should be tested for punctures, tears, and signs of perishing by stretching it gently, piece by piece, so that a section of 1 in. is extended to about 2 in. Chafing against the sides of the carrier (see page 43) is generally the cause of weaknesses here.

The thin rubber disc or valve fitted centrally to the stud on the inside end of the metal container should be soft, pliable, and flat. If it has become concave, it should be taken off the stud and reversed. If it has hardened, a new disc should be obtained from the local warden or A.R.P. office.

The rubber band joining the facepiece of the General Civilian Respirator to the metal container should be perfectly fresh and elastic. If it shows

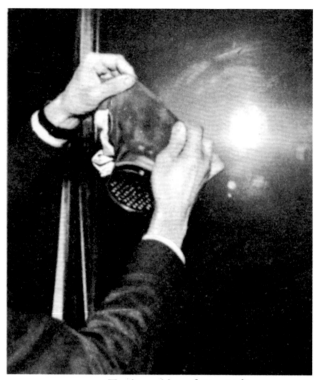

Testing rubber of gas-mask.

cracks, it is perishing and should be renewed. The container of the Small Child's Respirator screws into the facepiece and should be examined from time to time to see that it is tightly done up.

When moisture gets into the container, it discolours the white filter material visible through the air holes at the outer end of the container. If this happens, or if the container becomes dented or perforated, the gas mask must be handed in for examination as soon as possible to a local warden or other A.R.P. official.

How to Clean a Gas Mask.

A sponge or cloth should be dipped in a strong solution of toilet soap and warm water and thoroughly wrung out so that it is damp, but not dripping, and with this the gas mask or helmet should be swabbed over, inside and out. It should then be wiped with a clean, damp, but not dripping, cloth. Soap with soda in it must not be used, and care must be taken not to let moisture drip into the inside of the respirator.

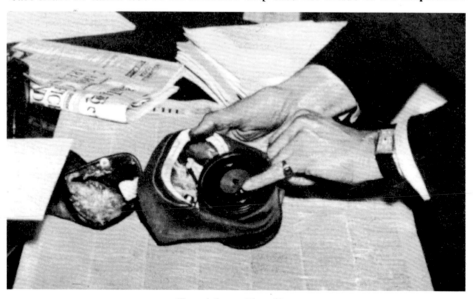

Examining rubber disc.

Always after use the inside of the facepiece should be wiped dry before the gas mask or helmet is put away.

Misting of the eyepiece is caused by condensation of the breath, and can be prevented by smearing the inside of the eyepiece with a thin film of good toilet soap before the gas mask is put away.

After exposure to blister gas vapour a gas mask must be thoroughly aired. If the mask is contaminated by liquid blister gas it must be returned at once to the local A.R.P. authority, who will issue another in its place.

Gas Mask Carriers.

Gas masks easily become unserviceable if they get crushed, or are exposed for a long time to heat or wet. When not in use they should be kept in a carrier in a cool, dry place. They should never be hung from the harness straps, nor carried loose in an attache case or soft fabric bag.

The Government issues a suitable cardboard carrier with each Civilian Gas Mask. Various alternative gas-mask carriers may be bought, but they should be chosen very carefully. The requirements of a satisfactory gas-mask carrier are these :—

(1) The carrier must be designed so that the gas-mask canister has to be at the bottom and the facepiece lies full length and flat on top. The canister must not be inverted on the facepiece and the facepiece must not on any account be turned inside out.

(2) The carrier must be rigid enough to protect the gas mask from being crushed, for instance, in a crowd or against a seat in an omnibus.

(3) The carrier must be smooth inside, with no rim or other projection to catch against the edge of the eyepiece.

(4) The gas mask in the carrier must not be a very loose fit, otherwise the carrier will abrade the rubber of the mask.

(5) If the carrier is part of a holdall or handbag, the owner must be able to get at the gas mask without having to remove other things first.

Whether a carrier is separate or not, no other article such as a first-aid outfit, pot of anti-gas ointment No. 2, electric torch, lipstick or powder-case should ever be packed in with the gas mask.

A gas mask carrier which is not waterproof should be carried in a waterproof satchel. If this is used with the cardboard carton the flap of the satchel should be large enough to overlap the side of the carton so that rain cannot get underneath, and the flap should coincide with the lid of the carton and be fastened with press studs rather than tie-tapes, so that the gas mask can be got out in a hurry.

Cardboard cartons can be strengthened by adhesive tape, stuck on at the bottom joint, the corners, and the hinge of the lid. A carrying cord threaded outside the bottom of the carton prevents the bottom from slipping loose. A good quality oil paint (which should be applied on the outside of the carton only) will help to keep out the wet. Cardboard cartons should be wiped over with tepid soapy water to clean them.

Loss and Damage of Respirators.

As respirators are Government property, they are not replaced free except in special circumstances.

Gas masks and helmets lost during air raids are replaced free. Gas masks are replaced or repaired free for children at grant-aided schools, unless the local authority decides that the loss or damage was not due to fair wear and tear. No charge is made in any circumstance for the replacement or repair of gas masks belonging to children evacuated under the Government scheme, or people in receipt of public assistance or unemployment relief, or the dependent members of their families. Children under school age can have their gas masks replaced or repaired free on the same conditions as ordinary school children, but this does not apply to babies' gas helmets, which are regarded as the parents' responsibility.

Apart from exemptions, the charges for replacing respirators and parts of respirators are as follows :—

(1) *General Civilian Type Gas Mask.*

Complete respirator (including carton)	2s. 6d.
Facepiece	1s. 6d.
Container	1s.
Carton	2d.

(2) *Small Child's Gas Mask.*

Complete respirator (including carton)	3s. 6d.
Facepiece	2s. 6d.
Container	1s.
Carton	2d.

(3) *Baby's Anti-gas Helmet.*

Complete helmet (including carton)	25s.
Main frame (without tailpiece)	4s. 9d.
Adjustable tailpiece on frame	2s.
Supporting strap with webbing straps for attaching to main frame	2s.
Enveloping bag	11s. 6d.
Draw tape on bag	3d.
Bellows	1s. 6d.
Elbow connector	1s.
Valve unit (inside elbow)	9d.
Container	1s.
Strap for securing the air unit to frame	3d.
Carton	6d.

In case of hardship some of the higher of these charges may be reduced.

It should be noted that the charges are for the loss of or damage to the old respirator. The newly issued or repaired respirator remains Government property and will have to be paid for in its turn if it also is lost or damaged.

Change of Address.

When people with babies' helmets or small children's gas masks move to a new address, they must leave the new address with the local A.R.P. authority of the district they are leaving and, on arrival at their new address, must get in touch with the nearest warden or A.R.P. office and state what babies' helmets or small children's gas masks they have and in what district they obtained them.

Anyone joining the Forces must take his civilian respirator with him and give it up in exchange for a Service respirator.

VI. How to Make a Gasproof Room.

To make a shelter or ordinary room gasproof, it is necessary to block up all openings through which air can enter. Layers of brown paper should be pasted over cracks in walls and floors, and over ventilators, and over the cracks between frames and windows. Other places can be plugged with tightly rolled newspapers or pieces of felt, or with a mush made by soaking newspaper in water. There are also a number of anti-gas plastic materials sold for this purpose.

Larger openings, such as chimneys, should be blocked up tightly with cloth bags or sacks, filled with newspaper or old rags. Spaces under doorways should be blocked up.

To make a room gas-proof means of course to make it for ordinary purposes untenantable, because it cannot be properly ventilated. In small houses where this would present a space problem, the materials for gasproofing might be held in readiness but applied only if it seemed that gas was about to be used.

It should be remembered that the gas-tightness of a room may be impaired by the effects of high explosives, so that a gas mask is necessary even in a gas-proof room (see p. 32).

VII. Animals and Poison Gas

Although animals are immune from the effects of tear gases and very little affected by nose gases, they are affected in much the same way as human beings by the more dangerous lung and blister gases; and animals contaminated by blister gas can spread contamination.

None of the various animal gas masks now being marketed is entirely satisfactory.

In air raids in the country it will generally be preferable to accept any gas risk and to leave animals in the open rather than in stables. If stables or sheds have to be used, they can be made gasproof by the methods described above for a gasproof room. Horses caught in a gas attack can get some protection from a wet nosebag or blanket tied round the nose and mouth.

For smaller animals, it is an easy matter to make a kennel gasproof by sealing cracks with putty and providing a tight-fitting door. A cat, dog, or other small animal will be fairly safe in a large cupboard or box, sealed as suggested above. A dog of 50 lb. can safely be kept in a closed box of 35 cubic feet for about two hours.

Gas-contaminated animals should not be touched except by qualified people.

Below: How to seal up a door in your gas-proof refuge room, using a blanket. This illustration comes from *Air Raid Precautions,* 1938.

CHAPTER 6
SIMPLE FIRST AID
Introductory.

The Services which deal with casualties caused by air raids include First Aid or Stretcher Parties, the Ambulance Service, First Aid Posts, First Aid Points, and various types of hospitals.

Any slightly injured person requiring treatment should go, if he is able, to the nearest First Aid Post or First Aid Point. Those more seriously injured will be given first aid by First Aid Parties, who will arrange, where necessary, for their removal to a First Aid Post or hospital.

After heavy raiding, there may be occasions when the services of first aid parties are not immediately available at all places where they are required. In such circumstances, simple measures taken quickly by people on the spot may prevent serious injury or even save life, as, for example, in cases of extreme hæmorrhage (bleeding) or of true asphyxia (suffocation). Some of the elements of First Aid are described here to enable those at the scene of an incident to help casualties while trained parties are on their way.

Wound Shock.

Every injury, unless trivial, may be followed by a condition known as Shock (or " Wound Shock "), which is a failure of vitality varying in degree from transient faintness to extreme and dangerous prostration. Shock is likely to be very marked amongst air raid casualties, and may even affect persons *who are otherwise uninjured.*

The condition can be divided into two stages : Primary Shock, which immediately follows the injury, and Secondary Shock, which may develop later as a result of pain or bleeding or cold for a prolonged period, or through clumsy or incorrect handling. If proper care is not taken, Primary Shock may lead to Secondary Shock, and this, if allowed to develop, is dangerous to life.

Primary Shock can be treated and Secondary Shock to a large extent prevented, by simple means :—

(i) Pain must be relieved; for example, by gentle adjustment of the casualty's position, or by suitable support to the injured part before removal.

(ii) The patient must be protected from chill, since in cases of Shock body temperature falls rapidly. Unnecessary removal of clothing should be avoided, and the casualty should be wrapped in blankets or coats with at least one layer between him and the ground.

(iii) Loss of blood must be checked.

(iv) Fractures or badly injured limbs or joints should be secured.

(v) Gentleness and smoothness are always essential in handling, lifting, and removing the patient.

(vi) Warm, sweet drinks, such as sweetened tea, are of advantage to patients suffering from Shock, but it is dangerous to give any drink or food to an unconscious person, or to one who has a wound in the belly, or who complains or gives evidence of abdominal pain.

Hot water bottles are useful for protecting a casualty from chill. They should be placed where they can best warm the circulating blood, for example, between the body and outspread arms, or across the upper part of the thighs, since in each of these regions main arteries are relatively close to the surface and the warmth is circulated through the body by means of the blood stream. Care should be taken, by wrapping the hot water bottles in woollen or other material, to avoid burning the patient. They should never be laid directly on the bare skin.

Where a domestic hot water bottle is not available, an ordinary glass bottle, or similar container, wrapped in any piece of material or article of clothing, will make a suitable substitute. If an ordinary glass bottle is used, it should be filled with warm, but not with boiling, water, especially if the bottle is cold, otherwise it may crack and subsequently break. In moving the casualty, care must be taken to prevent the bottle from being broken and the casualty cut.

Bleeding (Hæmorrhage)

Profuse bleeding from a large artery immediately endangers life. Loss of blood is in any case one of the main causes of both Primary and Secondary Shock, and even the continued oozing of blood from an extensive area of the body may lead, if neglected, to collapse and finally to death.

Types of Hæmorrhage.

Hæmorrhage may be either external, in which case it is easily discovered, or it may be internal, caused by injury to blood vessels inside the body, from which the blood escapes into internal organs or cavities of the chest or abdomen. In the latter case, no blood is visible externally, unless it is coughed up or vomited.

Symptoms of Hæmorrhage.

The signs and symptoms of severe uncontrolled bleeding, either external or internal, are as follows :—

(i) There is rapid loss of strength, accompanied by giddiness and faintness, especially if the patient is raised to a sitting or standing position.

(ii) The face and lips become pallid, and the skin cold and clammy.

(iii) Breathing becomes hurried and laboured, and may be accompanied by gasping, yawning, and sighing.

(iv) The pulse quickly becomes so weak and rapid as not to be felt at the wrist.

(v) The patient becomes thirsty.

(vi) He may become restless and throw his arms about or tug at clothing round the neck, unlike a patient suffering from Shock without serious bleeding, who will normally lie very still and quiet.

(vii) Finally, the patient may become wholly unconscious.

If these signs are observed, but no external cause is apparent, the case should be regarded as one of severe internal hæmorrhage.

Treatment of External Hæmorrhage.

Blood escapes with less force if the patient is sitting and still less if he is lying, than if he is upright, and the position of a casualty with external hæmorrhage should be adjusted accordingly. Except in the case of a fractured limb, the bleeding part should, where possible, be raised above the level of the heart, to lessen the flow of blood to it. Firm and even bandaging with a pad of cotton wool or other soft material placed over the wound will normally check the bleeding.

Bleeding from a severely lacerated limb should be dealt with by bandaging over a splint even though no fracture has been recognised.

Treatment of Internal Hæmorrhage.

Internal hæmorrhage can be treated only on the operating table. The first aid urgently needed is warmth, extremely gentle handling and lifting, and rapid but smooth removal for surgical attention. Where there is even a suspicion of internal hæmorrhage, the patient should on no account be allowed to eat or drink.

Wounds in the Abdomen.

Casualties with penetrating wounds in the abdomen are more comfortable and less liable to further damage in moving if they are placed on the back. If there is a gash or tear in the abdominal wall that runs vertically (lengthwise to the body), the head and shoulders should be kept low and the legs straight. If the gash runs horizontally (across the body), or if the wound is in the nature of a round hole, the abdominal wall should be relaxed by bending the knees over a box, haversack, or rolled coat, and slightly raising the patient's head and shoulders.

If any organs protrude, no attempt should be made to replace them. The abdominal wall being kept relaxed, as above, the organs should be covered with lint, a soft towel, cotton wool, clean soft flannel, or similar material, and the covering secured firmly, but not too tightly, with a broad bandage.

It is desirable for the material used in contact with the wound to be wrung out in warm water to which, if it is readily available, table salt may be added in the proportion of one teaspoonful of table salt to a pint of clean hot water.

On no account should a patient with an abdominal wound be given anything to eat or drink.

Fractures.

Simple Fractures.

When bone is fractured (broken) and the surrounding skin is undamaged, the injury is a simple fracture.

Compound Fractures.

When bone is broken and in addition there is a (flesh) wound at the site of the fracture, the fracture is said to be compound.

Complicated Fractures.

When bone is broken, and in addition there is damage to some important organ or structure, the injury is a complicated fracture.

The following signs and symptoms may be present in cases of fracture :—

(i) Pain at or near the point at which the bone is broken.

(ii) Loss of power of movement in the affected limb.

(iii) Swelling around the part affected.

(iv) Deformity, the limb falling into an unnatural position and having an abnormal shape. It may be shortened by the over-lapping of the broken ends of the bone.

(v) Irregularity; if the bone is close to the surface, a lump may be felt at the break and, if the fracture is compound, the bone may be exposed and visible.

Simple First Aid Treatment of Fractures.

    (i) The first object is to prevent further damage being done by injudicious movement or by careless handling, and especially to avoid converting a simple fracture into a compound one, or causing an uncomplicated fracture to become complicated.

    (ii) Unless the circumstances are such that danger to life is threatened, or that there is danger of further injury being caused if the patient is not immediately removed, the fracture should be attended to where the patient lies. The injured limb should be secured by splints or in some other way, and then the patient may be carefully moved.

    (iii) If there is severe bleeding which is immediately endangering life, this must be controlled first.

    (iv) Warmth and air are required to guard against shock which will certainly accompany the fracture. Blankets or coats should be wrapped round the patient, care being taken not to disturb him unduly. Merely covering the patient is not enough to prevent him from becoming chilled.

    (v) The limb should be placed in as natural a position as possible, with great care and without using force.

    (vi) If there is no material for splinting, a fractured leg may be secured by careful bandaging to the opposite leg or a fractured arm by bandaging to the trunk. If nothing else is available, filled sandbags may be used to keep an injured limb in position, until proper treatment is given.

    (vii) Splints real or improvised, must be sufficiently firm, and long enough to keep the joints immediately above and below the fracture at rest. The bandages must be firm, but not so tight as to interfere with the circulation of the blood.

    (viii) Splints should be put on over the clothing and should if practicable, be padded in places where there is risk of rubbing or where there would be gaps between the splint and the body. Any suitable material which is available, such as clothing, handkerchiefs, or newspaper may be used as padding.

Improvised Splints.

Serviceable splints may be improvised from such things as wooden laths, rifles, walking sticks, pieces of wood or cardboard, rolled up linoleum or newspaper, and a number of other articles, provided that the resulting improvisation gives sufficiently rigid support for the limb, and is long enough to prevent movement of the joints immediately above and below the fracture.

Improvised Bandages for Securing Splints.

Where the proper bandages, such as a triangular bandage, cannot be obtained, scarves, or other pieces of cloth can be used. Ties, braces, straps, belts or lengths of rubber tubing may be employed to secure splints or dressings.

Artificial respiration—backward swing.

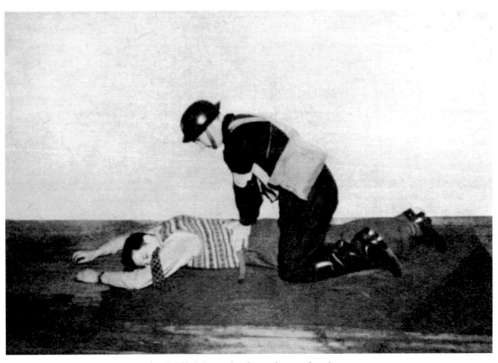

Artificial respiration—forward swing.

74

Improvised Slings.

Slings for a fractured arm or hand may be improvised by pinning the coat sleeve across the front of the garment, or by turning up the lower edge of the coat over the injured limb and pinning it to the lapel. A fractured arm can also be supported by carefully placing the hand inside the opposite lapel of the buttoned-up coat. Scarves, ties, or belts slung around the neck will also provide effective support for an injured arm or hand.

Unconsciousness (Insensibility).

As a general rule, an insensible person should be laid on his back, wrapped in coats or blankets, with the head turned to one side; if he has false teeth, they should be removed. If the face is flushed, the head and shoulders should be slightly raised; if the face is pale, the head and shoulders should be kept low. Any tight clothing, especially at the neck, chest, or waist should be loosened. Nothing must be given through the mouth to a person who is partly or wholly insensible. If an insensible person must be moved, smoothness and care are essential.

Suffocation (Asphyxia).

Anything which prevents the body from getting sufficient oxygen will cause a condition known as asphyxia, which, if unrelieved, will lead to insensibility and death.

Common causes of asphyxia under air raid conditions include continued pressure on the chest, for example, by debris; obstruction of the upper breathing passages by dust and dirt; confinement in a poisoned atmosphere (for instance, in an enclosed space containing domestic coal gas, exhaust fumes or after-damp); drowning, and electrocution.

The first action is to remove the cause of the asphyxia, or to move the casualty from the cause, whichever is the more suitable, and then immediately to begin artificial respiration, preferably by the Schafer method, which is as follows :—

The patient should be placed face downwards with his head turned to one side and his arms forward. The helper should kneel beside the patient facing towards the head and should place his hands on the small of the back, with wrists nearly touching, thumbs together and fingers passing over the loins on either side. He should swing rhythmically backwards and forwards from the knees at the rate of about twelve double-swings per minute, keeping his arms straight, so that his weight presses the patient's abdomen against the ground and forces his abdominal organs against his diaphragm on the forward swing, pressure being entirely released on the backward swing. The pressure period should occupy two seconds and the period of relaxation three seconds; to ensure regularity the rescuer should count evenly up to five on each double swing. This should be continued until natural breathing returns, when the rhythmic swing of the helper should coincide with the patient's respiratory movements.

Artificial respiration may have to be continued for an hour or longer, relays of helpers being employed if necessary.

While artificial respiration is being applied, other helpers should undo the casualty's tight clothing and wrap coats or blankets round him.

Removal from Electrical Contact.

In cases of injury due to an electric current, the current should, if possible, be switched off at once. If this is not possible, the helper must protect himself from becoming electrocuted, and to do this he must place some *dry* non-conducting material between himself and an earth. Non-conducting materials include *dry* rubber, linoleum, wood, glass, clothing and paper.

The injured person may be dragged away from the electric medium with a hooked walking stick or a loop of dry rope; an umbrella should not be used since the metal parts will conduct electricity. Metal and moisture are good conductors of electricity, and therefore the helper should avoid touching the hands, armpits, wet clothing, nailed boots, or metal equipment of the electrocuted person.

Burns (other than from Poison Gas) and Scalds.

A burn is caused by dry heat, for example by a flame, by hot metal, or by a strong acid or alkali. A scald is caused by wet heat, for example by steam, boiling water, or boiling oil.

General rules for the treatment of all burns or scalds are :—

(a) Air should be excluded from the affected part as soon as possible. The part should be covered with clean lint, soft clean cloths or cotton wool, and then bandaged. These are only temporary measures to meet the situation until suitable first aid dressings are prepared.

(b) Clothing should not be removed, unless absolutely necessary. If garments must be taken off, great care should be used. If the material sticks, it is necessary to cut around the pieces of cloth which adhere to the flesh so as to leave them in position when the garments are removed. If blisters have formed, they must not be broken or punctured, but should as far as possible be protected and kept intact.

(c) Suitable first aid dressings may be made from strips of lint or linen about 2 inches wide; they should be either :—

(i) soaked in a lotion made by stirring baking soda in clean water (about 2 teaspoonsful to a pint). The strips must be kept wet by repeatedly pouring the lotion over them without removing them from the burn.

or (ii) smeared with sterile white vaseline on the surface to be applied to the skin.

The dressings, which should be put on so as to overlap one another, should be covered with cotton wool or soft cloths and lightly bandaged, and the affected part supported.

When burns are severe or extensive, shock will be marked. The patient must be kept warm; fluids, such as hot sweet drinks, should be given in quantity. Oil and grease must not be applied to scalds or burns.

Summary.

In First Aid the primary consideration must always be to deal with immediate danger to life. Examples of such dangers are excessive bleeding, interference with normal breathing (through pressure on the chest, obstruction of the air passages by debris or electrocution), and nearness to moving machinery, tottering buildings, a spreading fire, or a poisoned atmosphere. In all such cases the source of danger must be removed from the casualty or the casualty moved away from the source of danger. After dealing with immediate danger to life, the second consideration is to try to avert or minimise injury, and the third to reduce pain and shock and make the casualty as comfortable as possible.

It may be convenient to sum up briefly some of the main guiding principles in elementary first aid :—

(i) Severe bleeding should be attended to at the earliest possible moment. This does not mean that every cut or wound should have prior attention. Discrimination should be used: the rule applies to profuse bleeding, the continuance of which would endanger life.

(ii) The casualty must be able to breathe normally. Any cause of difficult breathing must be dealt with, and artificial respiration, if needed, must be started promptly and maintained.

(iii) In cases of gross injury to a limb, whether or not a fracture is recognised, and in all cases of injury involving joints, the affected part should be supported and secured by simple methods before the casualty is moved, unless for any reason his life is in danger.

(iv) Anyone who is, or has been, buried under debris must be treated on the assumption that the severest crush injuries have been received. These might include fracture of the thigh, pelvis, or spine.

(v) A person who is wholly or partly unconscious, or one who is even suspected of suffering from internal injury, must not be given anything to eat or drink.

(vi) The indiscriminate use of alcohol in first aid can be dangerous; it should not be given except on the direct order of a doctor.

(vii) All seriously injured people will be suffering from Primary Shock. Secondary Shock, coming on some time after injury, may be fatal. Secondary Shock can, to a large extent, be prevented by the simple measures mentioned in this chapter; it may be brought on or made worse by rough handling and clumsy movement.

(viii) Chill should always be prevented, and the casualty should always be handled with the greatest care and gentleness.

Notes on Improvised Splints.

When proper splints are not available, it is usually possible to improvise suitable substitutes in a number of different ways, which will at least serve temporarily while trained persons with proper equipment are on their way. A few examples showing how articles in common use may be made to serve as improvised splints are given in the illustrations which follow.

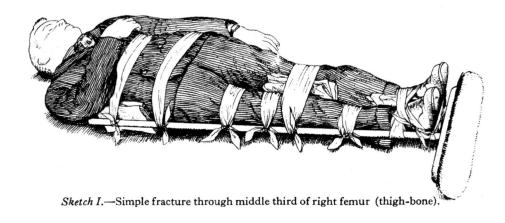

Sketch I.—Simple fracture through middle third of right femur (thigh-bone).

A broom used as a thigh splint by placing the handle along the injured limb, with the head of the broom at the feet. Loosely folded pieces of newspaper or other material may be used as padding, placed between the ankle and knee joints, and also at the hip.

Folded triangular bandages are shown in the illustration, but the improvised splint may be secured by any other material of sufficient length, such as, for example, neck-ties, belts, or scarves.

If sufficient bandages are not available to immobilise a fractured thigh in the manner here illustrated, the essentials are to bandage above and below the fracture and to ensure that the limb is kept rigid.

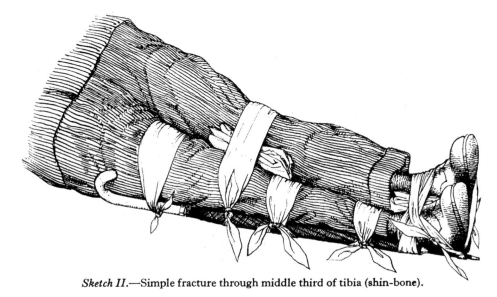

Sketch II.—Simple fracture through middle third of tibia (shin-bone).

The illustration shows an umbrella used as a splint. The ankles and knee joints are padded with loosely folded newspaper.

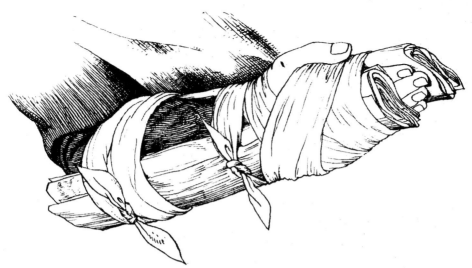

Sketch III.—Simple fracture through one or both bones of the forearm.

The illustration shows the use of newspaper, folded to the appropriate size of an arm splint, so as to be stiff enough to give rigid support.

Treatment of Gas Casualties. See pages 33-35.

IN CASE YOU BECOME A CASUALTY.

Always carry your Identity Card and with it a piece of paper giving the name and address of your nearest relatives or friends, and, in particular, of any near relative in the Forces whom you wish to be informed.

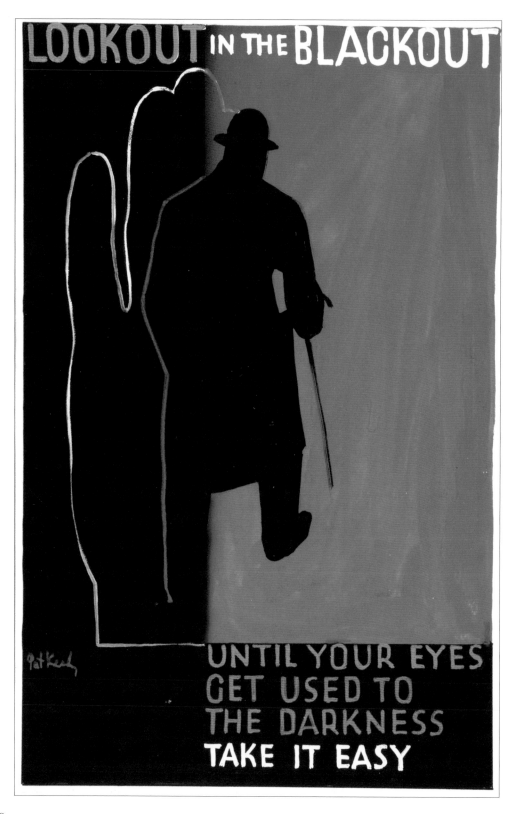

CHAPTER 7.

LIGHTING RESTRICTIONS.

The black-out is a vital part of our defence and to be effective it requires the intelligent co-operation of all. It is everyone's duty to know accurately the lighting restrictions that concern him, to attend carefully and cheerfully to advice or complaints from the wardens or police, and to notice the times of the black-out.

Most newspapers publish these times and it is worth observing that there are always two of them—the beginning of the black-out and the end. Some people tend to be most scrupulous about lighting restrictions at night when the black-out begins, and yet most careless about them in the early morning before the black-out is over.

Anyone who does not comply with the lighting restrictions is liable to a heavy fine or even imprisonment. The police have power to enter premises to deal with lights that contravene the law, and may order any light to be extinguished.

Lights from Houses and other Premises

All lights inside houses or other premises must be obscured during the black-out so that no light can be seen from outside.

Windows, skylights, fanlights, glazed doors and other light openings must be completely covered with dark curtains or blinds or other obscuring material such as stout paper or cardboard, so that no light shines through or shows round the edges. Curtains and blinds must be fastened so that they do not flap loosely in a draught and reveal light.

Screens of wood or wallboard or stout cardboard made to fit tightly into the window opening not only make an excellent black-out but give protection against flying glass.

All interior lights near outside doors must be screened so that no light can be seen from outside when the doors are opened. If necessary the door opening can be shielded on the inside with a semi-circular curtain or it can be boxed in with a light partitioning of plywood or cardboard.

Householders should examine their black-out from the outside at the back of the house as well as the front. It is best to black-out the whole of the house, except parts that are entirely unoccupied, during the black-out period.

Chimneys must be swept regularly, to prevent chimney fires, which would be a most useful beacon for enemy bombers.

Ventilating Blacked-out Rooms.

Blacked-out windows need not and should not mean stuffy rooms. There are various ways by which air can get into a room without light getting out.

The simplest method is to use enough extra black-out material to overlap the window opening for several inches all round, and to fix the black-out with rings or hooks so that it stands out from the wall. If the overlap of black-out material is not sufficient, strips of cloth or cardboard should be fixed round the edges of the window.

A more elaborate but more permanent method is to fit the window at the bottom with a ventilator light trap. This consists of a right-angular channel of wood or cardboard or sheet metal fixed to the bottom of the window so that air comes in underneath but light does not shine out. These traps are based on the principle that while air will circulate round corners, light will travel only in straight lines and is therefore easily obscured by a screen fixed at right angles to the way the light travels.

Window screens can easily be combined with a simple form of ventilator trap.

Full directions for making ventilator light-traps and for ventilating blacked-out rooms in other ways are given in the official leaflet " *Ventilation in the Black-out*," obtainable for a penny from H.M. Stationery Office or through a bookstall.

External Lighting.

Though the black-out has to be as black as possible, there are certain vital industries and other undertakings which cannot carry on without some external lighting during the black-out. Under conditions agreed with the Air Ministry, external lighting is allowed for railways, docks and certain industries. Some lights, such as railway signals, are left on after an Alert has sounded, but it has been proved by observation from the air that these lights can give no help to enemy pilots.

Except for lights specifically allowed, no external light may be shown during the black-out. A bonfire, for instance which remains alight after the black-out begins is an offence and the person responsible is liable to be prosecuted. Outside garage and porch lights, like other outside lights, are prohibited, and the electric bulbs should be removed so that the lights cannot be switched on by mistake.

Electric Torches and Hand Lamps.

Torches must not be used out-of-doors at any time during the black-out unless the light aperture has been reduced to not more than 1 inch in diameter (the size of a half-penny) and also dimmed by the insertion of a piece of newspaper or its equivalent (two pieces of tissue paper are not an adequate equivalent). The light must be white, and the torch must always be pointed downwards. It should never be flashed in the eyes of an oncoming driver, or a serious accident may result.

Correctly dimmed torches may be used after the Alert unless the police order them to be put out.

The hooded "A.R.P. hand-lamp" may be used by anyone until there is an Alert, and this lamp need not be dimmed like a torch; but after the Alert the hand-lamp may be used only by Civil Defence personnel or other people authorised by the police.

Until there is an Alert, hurricane lamps may be used on farms or for other kinds of work for which such lamps are necessary, but they must be kept as dim as possible, and screened so that no light goes upwards.

Shops and Places of Entertainment.

Ordinary shop window lighting and lights on stalls are prohibited during the black-out, but shops and places of entertainment are allowed to display small dimly illuminated signs. These must be placed inside a window or within a doorway, must be inconspicuous at 100 feet away, and must comply with the other conditions laid down in paragraph 40 of the Lighting (Restrictions) Order, 1940, as amended.

To prevent light being shown through doors when people go in and out, it is usually necessary to have some kind of light-lock for the door. Simple forms of light-locks are described in a specification, number BS/ARP 15, issued by the British Standards Institution.

Motor Vehicles and Motor Cycles.

Drivers of motor vehicles should inspect their lights frequently to make sure that they comply strictly with black-out requirements. Vehicles showing too much light may help enemy aircraft; but lights that are too dim may cause unnecessary accidents.

Side lights, rear lights,* and stop-lamps must be treated so that the aperture is one inch in diameter (the size of a half-penny), and so that the light is clearly visible at 30 yards, but invisible at 300 yards. It is important that the light should not become invisible at a distance much less than the prescribed 300 yards; otherwise oncoming drivers will not be able to see it. The lamp glass must be kept clean, so that visibility is not reduced by mud or dirt.

It is recommended that the lights should be treated as follows :—

(1) Apply black paint on the *inside* and *outside* of the front glass leaving clear a circle of 1 in. in diameter.

(2) Dim the 1 in. circle so that the light showing through it, while clearly seen at 30 yards, becomes invisible at 300 yards. This can be done in various ways, for example :—

> (a) By getting a garage or electrical firm to reduce the power of the bulbs by putting a resistance in the circuit.

> (b) By applying white paint on the inside of the clear space of the lamp glass.

> (c) By fitting one or more pieces of semi-opaque white paper or other suitable material inside the lamp glass.

> In the case of dual-purpose masks, the aperture, which serves as a side-light, should be reduced to the size of a half-penny, and its brightness reduced in the same way, so that when the lower-powered bulb is in use the light will be clearly visible at 30 yards but invisible at 300 yards.

> After obscuration, the lights should be tested on a level road at the prescribed distances, on a dark night when there is no moon.

> Rear-lights and stop-lights must not be more than 3½ feet from the ground. Two rear-lights and/or two stop-lights may be used.

Headlamps* are restricted to one headlamp for each vehicle (except on buses and coaches). The headlamp may be on either the near or off-side. The headlamp must be fitted with a mask of the prescribed type. The light output must not exceed 2.5 foot candles at 10 feet from the lamp. If the

---

* Under the Lighting (Restrictions) (Amendment) No. 3, Order of September 15, 1941, the use of *two masked headlamps* is now permitted. If you use a second headlamp it also must comply with the conditions given above. Your *rear light* need no longer be reduced as to aperture, and need only be dimmed by one sheet of tissue paper or equivalent. These improvements may only be temporary, and if you take advantage of them you must be ready to go back, at short notice, to the lower standard described above.

A.R.P. type of mask is used with a 36-watt lamp, there will usually be no risk of exceeding this.

The mask must be adjusted so that no light is thrown upwards on a level road. This can be tested by standing directly in front of the lamp and marking with the finger the point at which the top of the beam strikes the clothing; the light is not properly adjusted unless, at a distance of 10 or 12 paces, the beam strikes the clothing at or somewhat below the same point.

A masked headlight may be used after the Alert has sounded but must be put out when the vehicle is stationary (except when it is stopped for traffic reasons or at traffic lights) or on the instructions of the police.

*Combined head and side-lamps** fitted to motor-cycles and cars must use the prescribed "dual-purpose" mask on which the small aperture is 1 in. in diameter and is dimmed like an ordinary sidelight. If a motor vehicle has two such lights, one must be fitted with the regulation mask and the other have a small aperture 1 in. in diameter, in the same way as a side-lamp.

Fog lamps may be used during fog, provided they have the centre not more than $2\frac{1}{2}$ ft. above the ground. Alternatively, during fog an unscreened headlamp may be used. The light must be controlled by a separate switch and directed downwards and towards the nearside. The light must be switched off immediately on the direction of the police, or if the fog clears or if the Alert is sounded.

Direction indicators must be obscured except for a strip or arrow $\frac{1}{8}$ inch wide.

Bumpers and running boards (or equivalent positions) must either be painted white or have some white material applied to them.

Speed Limits.

During the black-out, vehicles are subject to a speed limit of 20 m.p.h. on all roads in built-up areas. The limit does not apply to fire, ambulance, or police vehicles on urgent business.

Pedal Cycles.

Cycles used during the black-out must carry a white front light, a red rear light and a white patch of not less than 12 sq. ins. on the back mudguard. The top half of the front glass of the front light and any side or rear panels must be completely obscured, and the bottom half of the reflector must be painted with matt black paint, or otherwise made ineffective. Any light showing through ventilation holes should be screened as far as possible. The red rear-light must be treated in the same way as the rear-light of a motor vehicle.

A cycle may be wheeled without lights, provided it is kept to the extreme left-hand side of the road.

A stationary cycle must have a red rear-light unless it is as near as possible to the left-hand side of the road.

Horse-drawn Vehicles and Handcarts.

Horse-drawn vehicles must have their front lamps obscured in the same way as cycle front lamps (see above). They must also carry red rear-lights fixed not higher than $3\frac{1}{2}$ feet from the ground, and these lights must be dimmed with one thickness of tissue paper or its equivalent.

* See under "headlamps." You may now use two lights, each fitted with a regulation "dual-purpose" mask.

A combined front and rear lamp may be used, provided that it is dimmed as described above for front lamps and provided no part of the vehicle or load extends more than 6 feet behind the lamp.

Handcarts which are required to carry front lamps must have the lamps dimmed similarly to cycle front lamps; and all handcarts must have a red rear-lamp dimmed with one thickness of tissue paper or its equivalent.

All such vehicles when on a road at night must have strips or patches of white paint (or other material equally conspicuous) on the front, back, and sides.

Animals.

Apart from animals being driven in vehicles or ridden, animals led or driven on a road during the black-out must have a white light carried in front of them. If there are more than four animals a white light must be carried behind as well. The light must be screened and dimmed so that no conspicuous light is thrown up or down.

In the BLACK-OUT

The Railways are giving as much light as they are permitted. You can make the black-out " lighter " if you—

- **Keep the blinds down.**
- **Tell your fellow passengers the names of the stations.**
- **Be sure your train is at the platform before alighting.**
- **Close the carriage door after you.**
- **Have your ticket ready at the barrier.**

RAILWAY EXECUTIVE COMMITTEE

Blackout restrictions were imposed on 1 September 1939, several days before the declaration of war. Doors and windows of buildings had to be covered with a suitable material, street lights were turned off or dimmed, and vehicle lights were fitted with slotted covers to divert their beams downwards. Inevitably there was an increase in accidents, among both drivers and pedestrians, as well as a rise in crime. This advertisement, shown right, was published by the Railway Executive Committee.

APPENDIX

TABLE OF WAR GASES

	1 Properties	2 Odour	3 Effects Upon Human Body	4 General Function of Group of Gases
Tear Gases C.A.P. .. .. (*Non-persistent.*)	Solid; used in particulate cloud, almost invisible.	Aromatic like floor polish.	Stinging of eyes, producing tears and spasms of eyelids. Slight skin irritation.	Mainly harassing agents producing temporary results; effective in very low concentrations.
B.B.C. .. .. (*Very persistent.*)	Yellowish-brown crystalline solid when pure, but probably used in brown liquid mixture. Invisible in gaseous state.	Penetrating bitter sweet smell.	Stinging of eyes, producing tears and spasms of eyelids. No skin irritation.	
Nose Irritant Gases. D.A. . . D.M. . . D.C. . . (*Non-persistent.*)	Crystalline solid of arsenical nature; D.A. and D.C. are colourless; D.M. is bright yellow when pure and greenish-brown when impure. When heated all give off a particulate cloud, which is generally invisible except near the point of release.	Practically odourless.	Burning sensation in nose, mouth, throat, and chest slightly delayed, accompanied by sneezing and mental depression.	Harassing agents with temporary results; effects felt after slight delay.
Lung Irritant Gases. Chlorine .. .. (*Non-persistent.*)	A greenish gas. It is a powerful oxydising agent, corroding metals swiftly and, more	Penetrating, like bleaching powder.	Coughing and watering of eyes; lung damage developing later.	

	Physical properties	Odour	Physiological effects	
Phosgene (*Non-persistent.*)	slowly, rotting clothing, especially in the presence of moisture. Almost invisible gas. Corrodes metal.	Like musty hay, producing suffocating sensation.	Ditto.	Lethal agents.
Chloro-picrin (*semi-persistent.*)	Colourless liquid, perhaps yellowish in use.	Similar to Chlorine.	Ditto. Has pronounced lachrymatory properties and produces vomiting.	
Blister Gases. Mustard (*Persistent.*)	An oily liquid heavier than water, varying from dark brown to straw-yellow. May produce iridescent stain. Emits invisible gas. Liquid and gas have great powers of penetration.	Likened by different people to garlic, onions, horseradish, or mustard. May be faint or pronounced.	Irritation producing inflammation in eyes and throat, possibly resulting in blindness and lung damage. Reddening and blistering of skin. Symptoms delayed, appearing from 2-8 hours or more after exposure.	Highly destructive to all living tissues.
Lewisite (*Persistent.*)	Colourless liquid when pure, but brown in crude state; heavier than water. Emits invisible gas. Liquid and gas have great powers of penetration. Contains arsenic.	When impure has strong smell of geraniums.	Severe irritation to nose and damage to eyes and lungs, possibly with permanent effects. Reddening and blistering of skin. Effects noticed immediately.	
Other Gases. Arseniuretted hydrogen (*Non-persistent.*)	Invisible gas.	Practically odourless.	Headache, nausea, and vomiting, with pain in the back and stomach. Severe symptoms do not usually develop till an hour or two after exposure.	Affects the blood, the liver and the kidneys.

SELECTION OF OFFICIAL PUBLICATIONS

The Air Raid Precautions Handbooks and Memoranda have been produced by the Ministry of Home Security with the assistance of the Government Departments and other bodies concerned.

The Handbooks are designed to describe a scheme of precautions which it is hoped will prove effective in preventing avoidable injury and loss of life, or widespread dislocation of national activities. They aim at giving the best available information on methods of passive defence against air attack, and are revised from time to time in the light of developments and experience.

The Memoranda deal with various aspects of the organisation to be provided by local authorities for public air raid precautions services.

HANDBOOKS.

No. 1. " **Personal Protection Against Gas** " (*2nd Edition*). **6d.** (8d.)

Gives rules of personal protection, and general knowledge of the nature and dangers of war gases.

No. 2. " **First Aid and Nursing for Gas Casualties** " (*3rd Edition*). **4d.** (5d.)

Provides information of both a general and technical nature required by nurses, first-aid parties, and the personnel of first-aid posts, to enable them to carry out their respective duties. Complementary to Handbook No. 1.

No. 4. " **Decontamination of Materials** " (*1st Edition*). **6d.** (8d.)

Explains the general principles governing the methods of counter-acting contamination arising from war gases. A text-book for the training of the members of decontamination services.

No. 4A. " **Decontamination of Clothing, including Oilskin Anti Gas Clothing, and Equipment from Blister Gases** " (*1st Edition*). **3d.** (4d.)

This Handbook may be regarded as supplementary to Handbook No. 4, in which it will eventually be incorporated. For this reason, the Handbook is provisional only.

No. 9. " **Incendiary Bombs and Fire Precautions** " (*1st Edition*). **6d.** (8d.)

This handbook, though written primarily for instructors, is designed also to serve as a general text-book on methods of dealing with incendiary bombs and the resultant fires. Demonstrates how the danger from incendiary bombs can be minimised, and why this can only be achieved with the co-operation of the general public and industry.

No. 10. " **Training and Work of First Aid Parties** " (*1st Edition*). **6d.** (8d.)

Concerns the organisation, training and work of First Aid Parties

No. 12. " **Air Raid Precautions for Animals** " (*1st Edition*). **3d.** (4d.)

Intended for the guidance of persons engaged in the care and management of animals.

MEMORANDA.

No. 1. " **Organisation of Air Raid Casualties Service** " (*2nd Edition*). **6d.** (8d.)

No. 2. " **Rescue Parties and Clearance of Debris** " (*3rd Edition*). **2d.** (3d.)

No. 3. " **Organisation of Decontamination Services** " (*2nd Edition*). **2d.** (3d.)

No. 4. " **Organisation of Air Raid Wardens' Service** " (*2nd Edition*). **2d.** (3d.)

No. 6. " **Local Communications and Reporting of Air Raid Damage** " (*2nd Edition*). **6d.** (8d.)

No. 11. " **Gas Detection and Identification Service** " (*2nd Edition*). **3d.** (4d.)

No. 12. " **Protection of Windows in Industrial and Commercial Buildings** " (*1st Edition*). **4d.** (6d.)

No. 13. " **Care and Repair of Respirators** " (*3rd Edition in the press*). **2d.** (3d.)

OTHER PUBLICATIONS.

" **Shelter at Home.**" **3d.** (4d.)

" **Ventilation in the Black-out** " (*Revised Edition*). **1d.** (2d.)

Prices are net. Prices in brackets include postage.

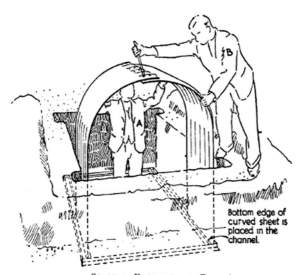

Bottom edge of curved sheet is placed in the channel.

STAGE 5. ERECTING THE BACK ARCH.
A. Supports curved sheets. B. Levers slots into line with bar.

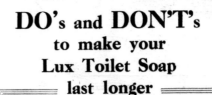

ADVERTISING IN WARTIME

Despite shortages of materials, the rationing and the disruption caused by the air raids, businesses still carried on throughout the war, making and selling chocolate, clothing, soaps and so on, although the range of products was tailored to some extent by the changing needs of the consumers. In October 1919, barely a month after the start of the war, the *Picture Post* published a statement aimed at reassuring its national advertisers:

> At a time like this, it is very natural that the minds of advertisers should be occupied with sterner things than advertising ... Can you blame the advertiser if he is bewildered and befogged? Let's wait till things settle down a bit, he says. Let's see what trade will be like in a month or two. And there he is, waiting for things to settle down rather than helping things settle down. Well, people have still got to eat, people will still have a free choice, people even still buy delicacies. Has he adapted his appeal to the changed conditions – to meet the needs of soldiers and ARP workers as well as housewives? Is he aware, for example, that women ambulance drivers and nurses and auxiliary territorials still care about their appearance – that he must produce new products for their new circumstances? And he must tell them about these new products.

In other words, it was time to 'Keep Calm and Carry On'. This selection of advertisements comes from a number of wartime magazines and newspapers.

The barrage balloons were a familar sight floating above London and many other cities and strategically important locations. Ever the butt of jokes, they featured in many advertisements and also in a series of children's books such as *Boo-Boo the Barrage Balloon*. The books were intended to make the silvery sentinels less frightening to the children.

THE WEEK'S
FOOD
FACTS № 12

PERHAPS you have been finding it difficult to sleep lately. A lot of people have. But a few commonsense rules of diet may make all the difference. Sleeplessness is very often caused by indigestion — so make your supper a light nourishing meal and try to eat it an hour or two before you go to bed. Then, last thing before you turn in, drink a glass of warm milk or cocoa. This will help you to get calm and restful sleep.

ON THE KITCHEN FRONT

How to make a Hay-Box

Hay-box cookery is particularly suitable for stews, soups, root vegetables, pulses, porridge and bacon.

A wooden box measuring about 2 ft. deep and 2 ft. 6 in. square is a convenient size. You can often buy one at your grocers. It must be fitted with a strong lid, secured with hinges and a hasp.

First line the box and lid with several thicknesses of newspaper; then, if you have it, with some clean, old flannel or felt. Use tacks to keep these linings in place.

Pack the box *tightly* with hay to within about 4 ins. of the top, making two nests in the hay for your cooking pans. A padding of hay should also be fixed to the underside of the lid.

Make a hay cushion 4 ins. thick to put on top of your pans.

To use the hay-box, bring your food to the boil in a pan on the stove, put on the lid tightly, then wrap the pan in newspaper and put it in one of the nests in the hay-box. Cover with the cushion, fasten the lid and leave the food to cook, allowing at least twice as long as for ordinary simmering. When required, heat up on the stove again before serving.

A SUPPER-TIME SWEET
Bird's Nest Pudding

Peel and core 4 or 5 large cooking apples but leave them whole. Fill the centres with sultanas. Arrange in a pie dish and sprinkle round them one tablespoonful of sago, and a dessertspoonful of sugar. Pour in half a pint of cold water, cover and bake in a moderate oven until the apples are quite tender. (About ¾ hour.)

Turn on your wireless at 8.15 every morning to hear useful hints and recipes

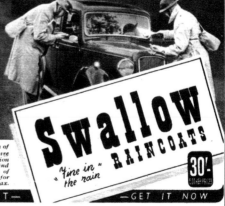

Picture Post, October 7, 1939

A minute for a stand-up meal!

You know what a wonderful food good chocolate is. Fry's Sandwich is the new chocolate discovery — the finest chocolate food that has been made yet. *It's all the very best of the best plain chocolate and all the best of the very best milk chocolate combined.* This delicious blend of milk and plain chocolate is real food, packed with quick energy and nourishment.

Get a supply now. Keep it by you. Take some with you wherever you go. It's handy to carry. It's easy to eat. *It's the perfect emergency ration.*

LAYER OF MILK
LAYER OF PLAIN
LAYER OF MILK

2d 2 OZ.
4 OZ. **4d**

RED LABEL — Double Milk (plain chocolate between two layers of milk).
BLUE LABEL — Milk (milk chocolate between two layers of plain).

FRY'S Sandwich Chocolate

D. 186. 13939

ACKNOWLEDGEMENTS

The material included in this book comes from various original wartime publications. Additional material/images are from the US Library of Congress, Campbell McCutcheon, and John Christopher's collection.

HOW TO SURVIVE AN
ATOMIC ATTACK

Also from Amberley Publishing, this companion volume to *Air Raids – What You Must Know, What You Must Do*! – uses official Cold War guidelines to show you how to build a shelter and survive an atomic attack.

Price £9.99 ISBN 978 1 4456 3997 0 (print), 978 1 4456 4008 2 (ebook)